Copyright

KDP Independent Publishing Platform

ISBN: 979-8571817684 (KDP-Assigned)

The content in this book meets the public domain requirements.
Differentiated works are unique illustrations.

*Le Onde by Ludovico Einaudi is a method of learning piano featuring
unique color-coded illustrations of sheet music called Piano Tab.
Play Piano by Letters translates musical notation by
replacing note symbols with letters.*

WARNING: Any duplication, adaptation or distribution of the expressions contained in this collection of intellectual property, without written consent of the owner, is an infringement of U.S. Copyright law and is subject to the penalties and liabilities provided therein.

Visit www.PlayPianoByLetters.com to see more piano tabs.
Check out our other books & rate us at Amazon.com
to receive a FREE piano tab song when you
Contact us on our website.

How to Read Piano Tab

This method of piano tab takes the note symbols out of sheet music and replaces them with letters.

- You read letters starting at the top and moving to the bottom of the page.

- A keyboard template is used as a guide, visible at the top of each page.

- Middle "C" is colored red or blue in the keyboard template header for easy reference on where to start the song.

- The rhythm count or beat is located in the left column along with each measure number and chords if needed.

- Notes played with the left hand are colored blue.

- Notes played with the right hand are colored red.

- As needed, fingering numbers are next to the note letters.

- When 2 or more notes are written horizontally, they are played together, indicated by a dotted line.

- A blue or red bold vertical line under a note letter represents a sustained count.

- A black "X" under a note letter represents a rest or staccato note.

Contents

Le Onde

Intro	1
Part 1	2
Part 2	4
Part 3	7
Part 4	11
Re-Intro	13
Part 5	15
Part 6	19
Part 7	21
Part 8	25
Part 9	27

La Linea Scura

Intro	29
Part 1	31
Part 2	35
Part 3	37
Part 4	41
Part 5	43
Part 6	49

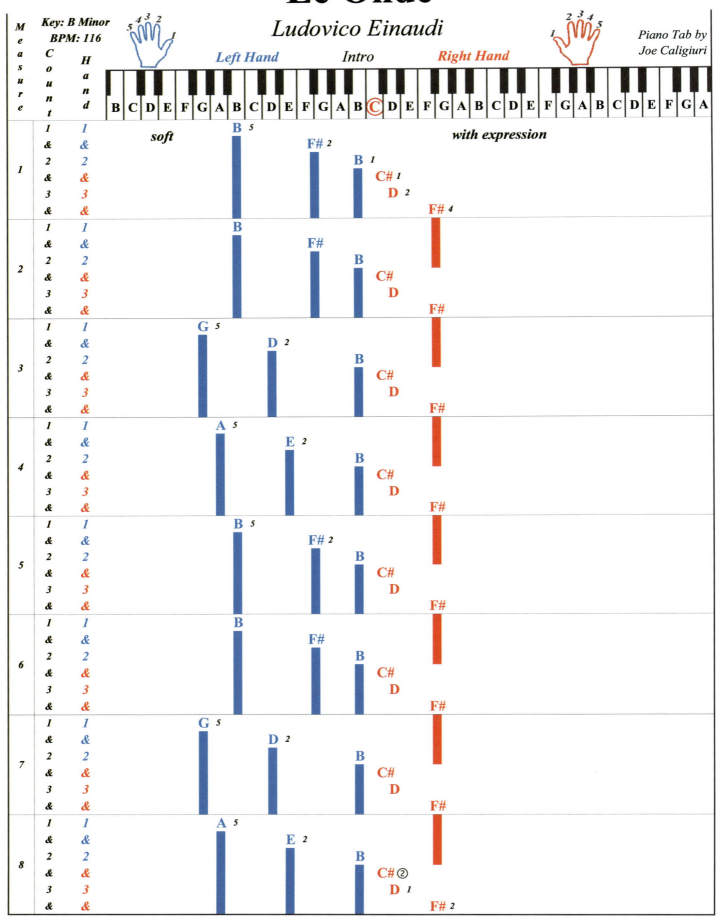

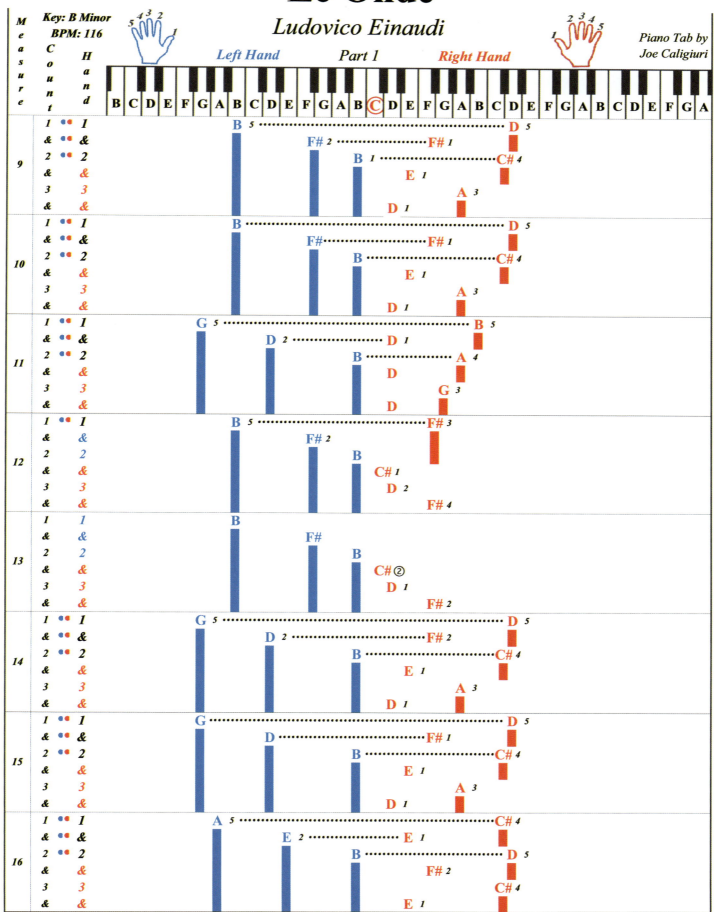

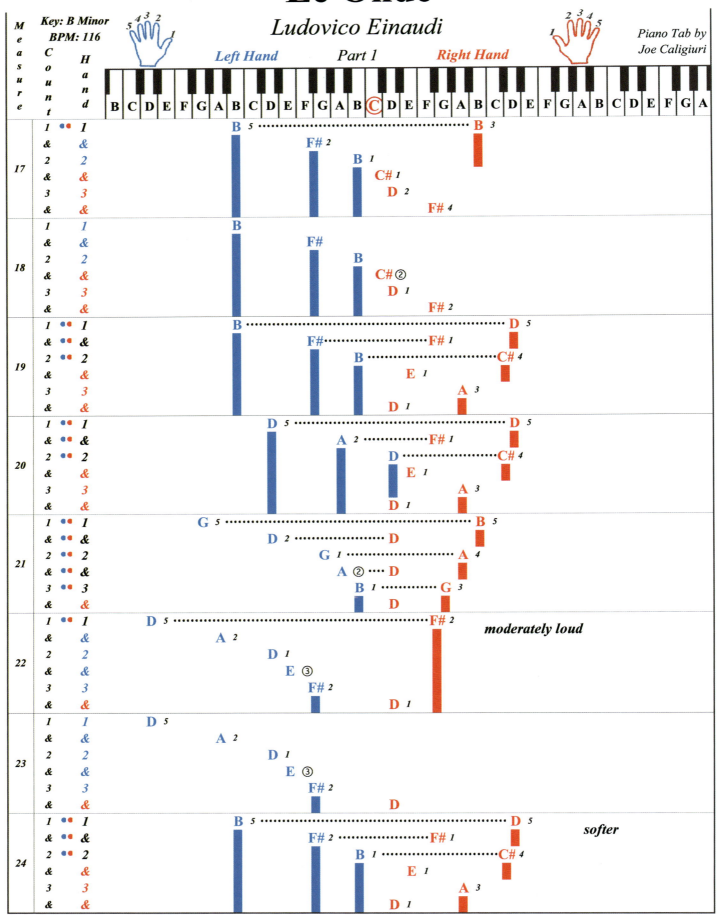

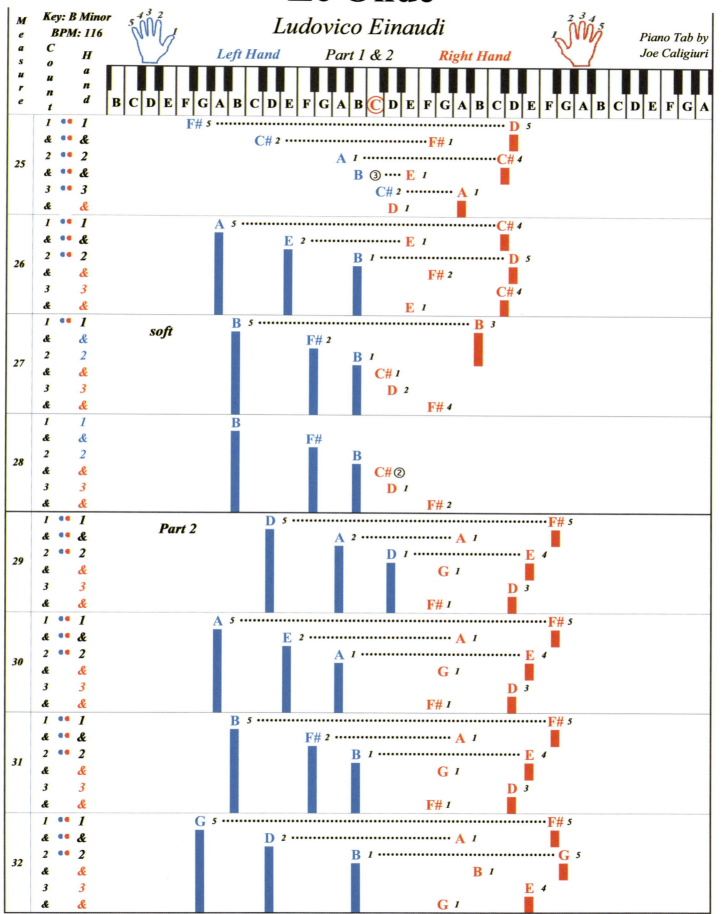

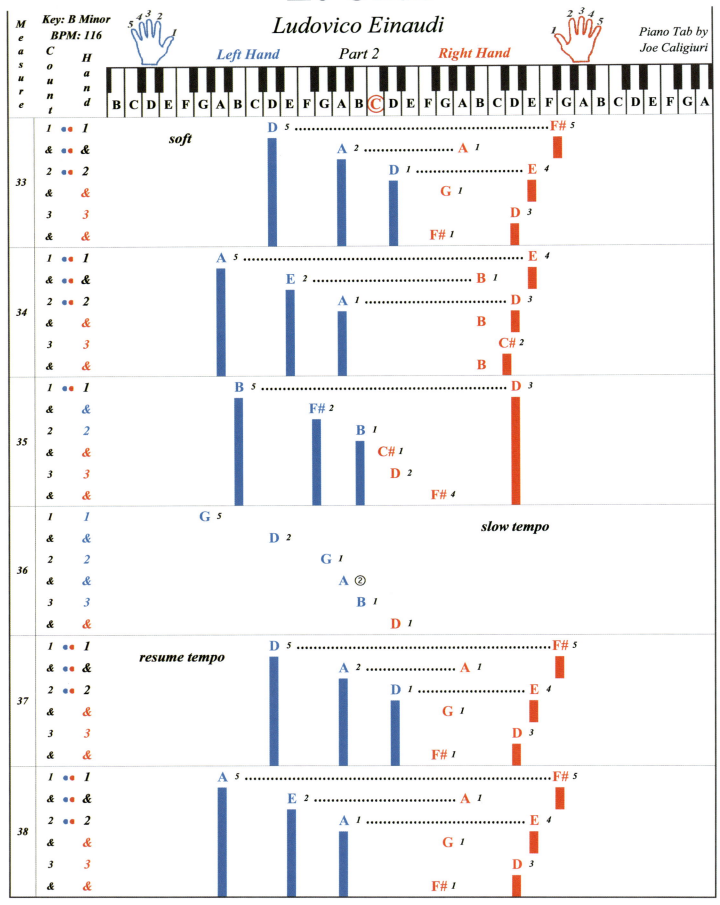

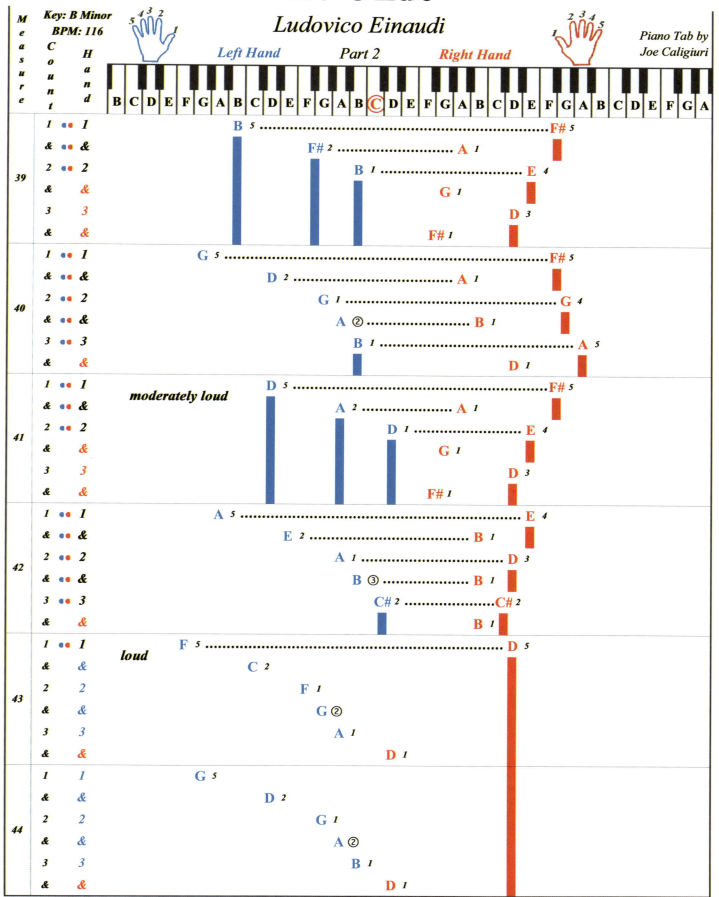

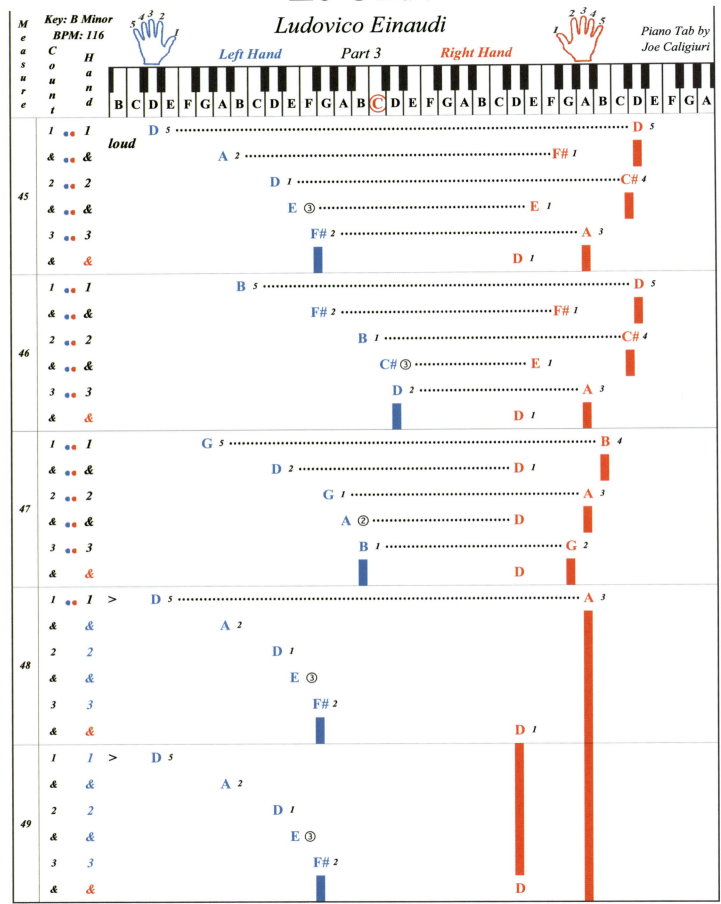

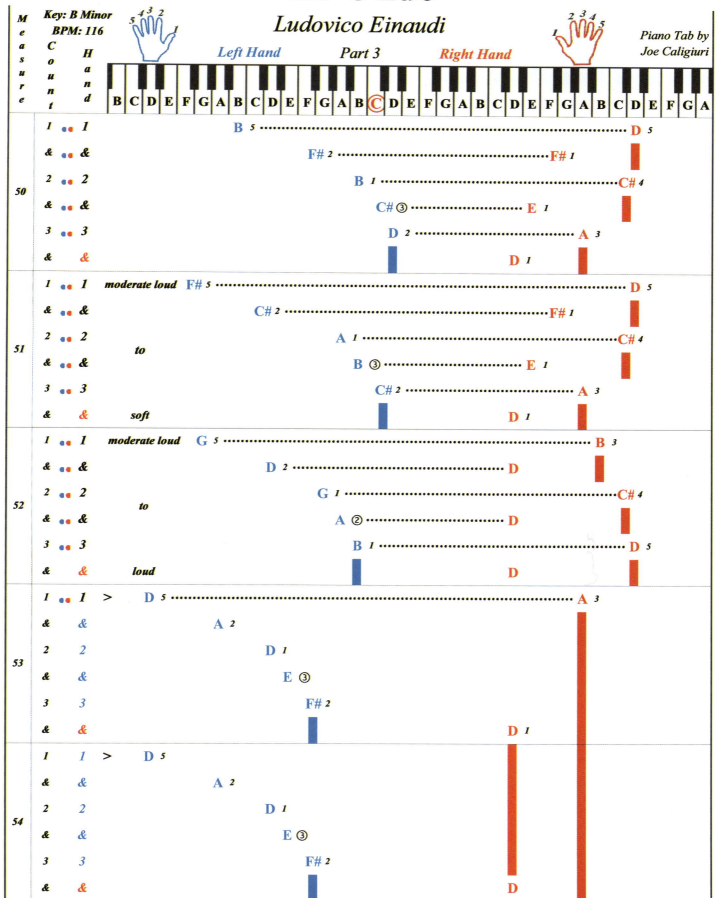

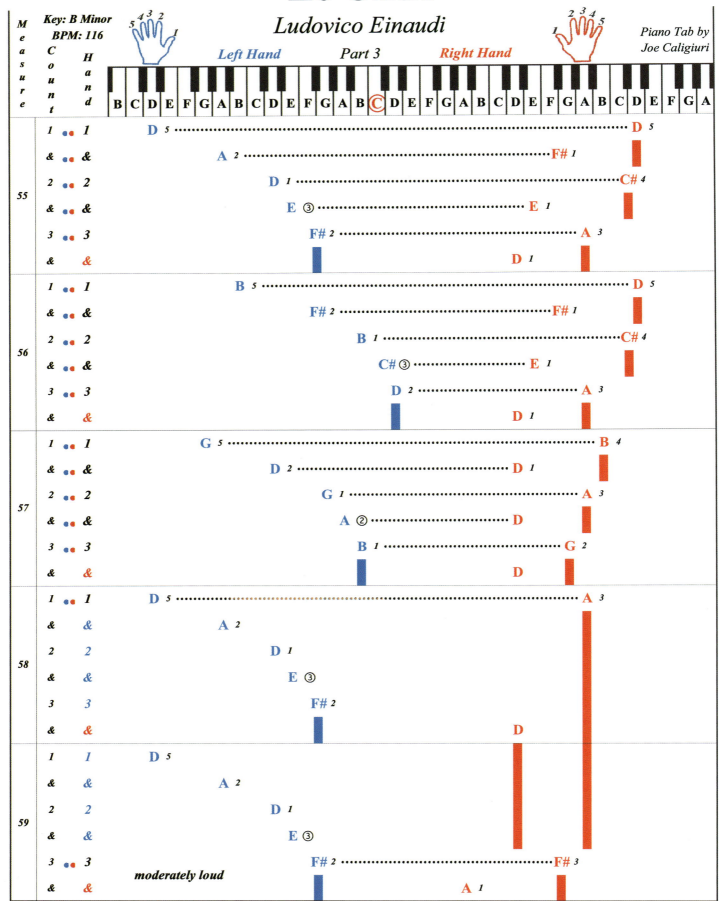

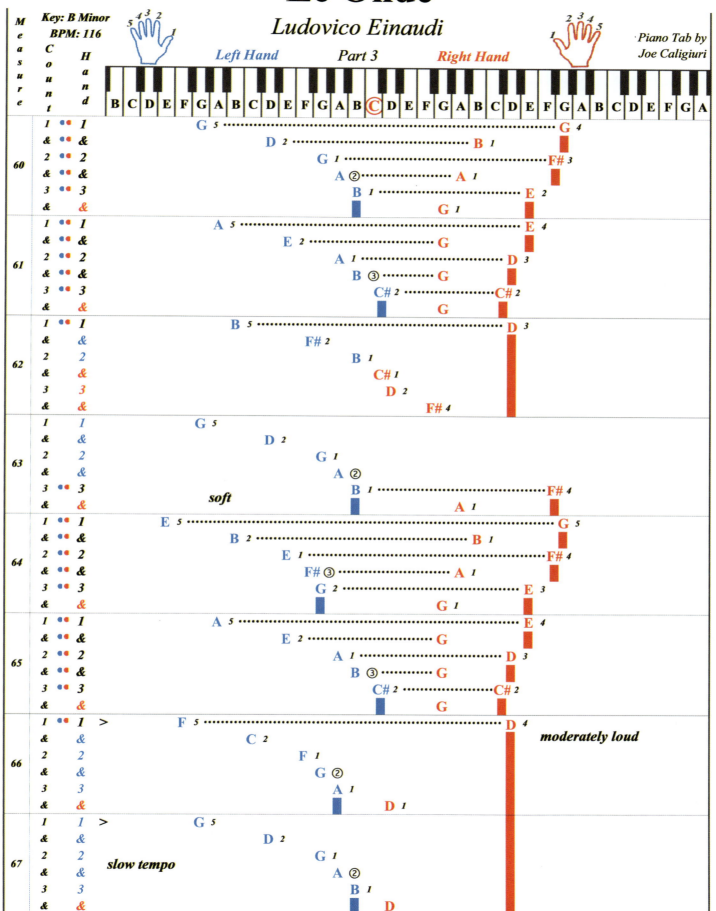

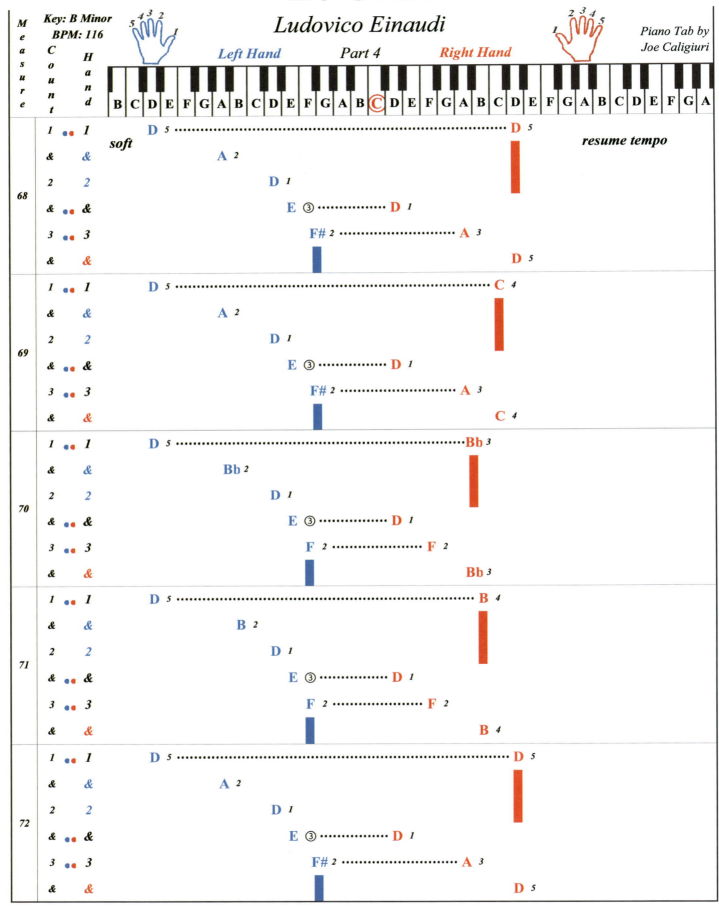

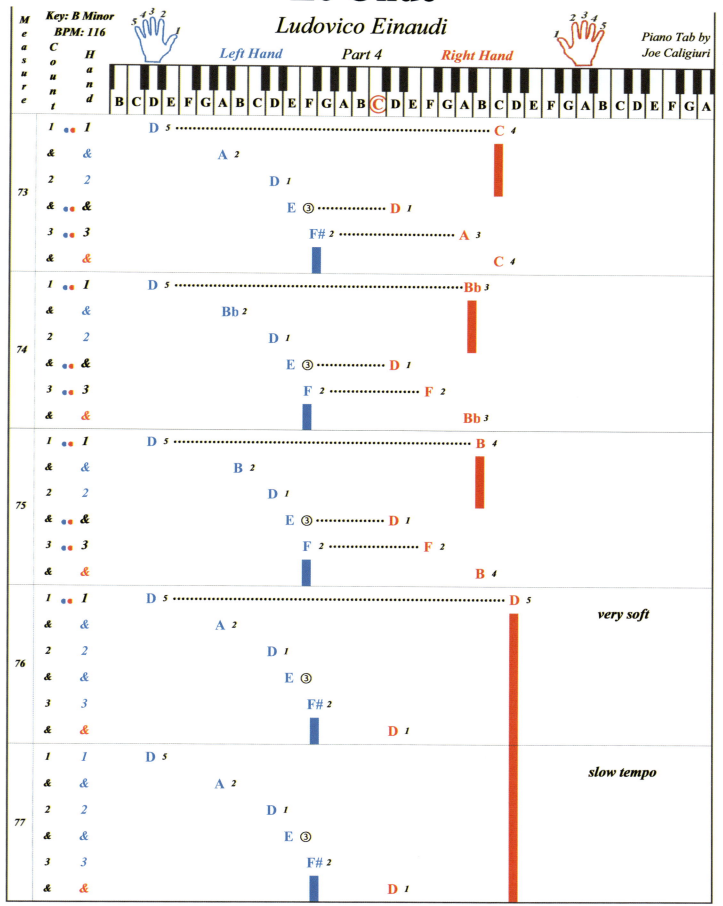

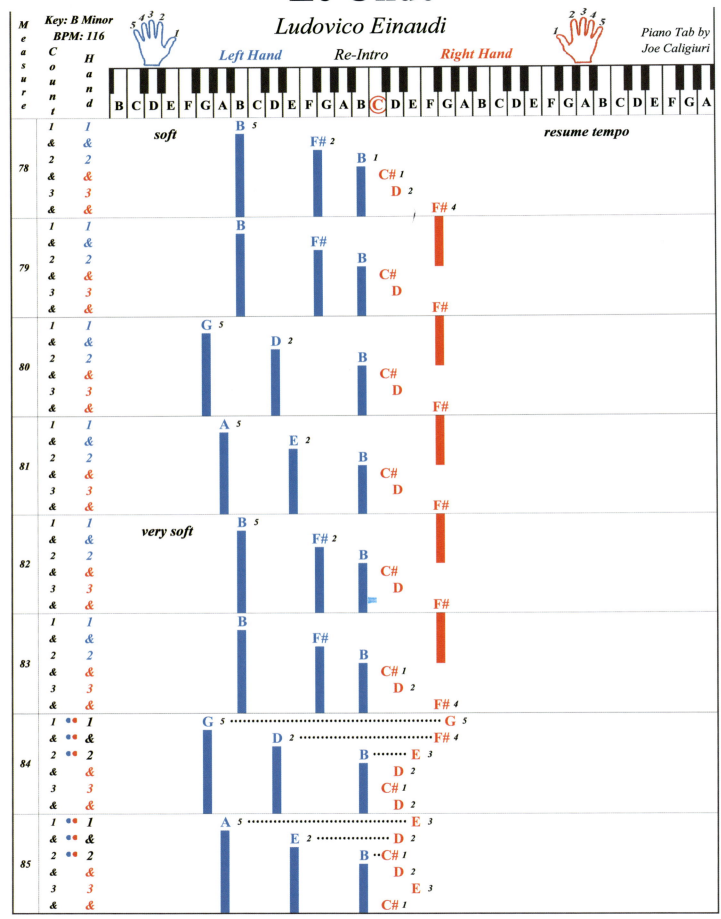

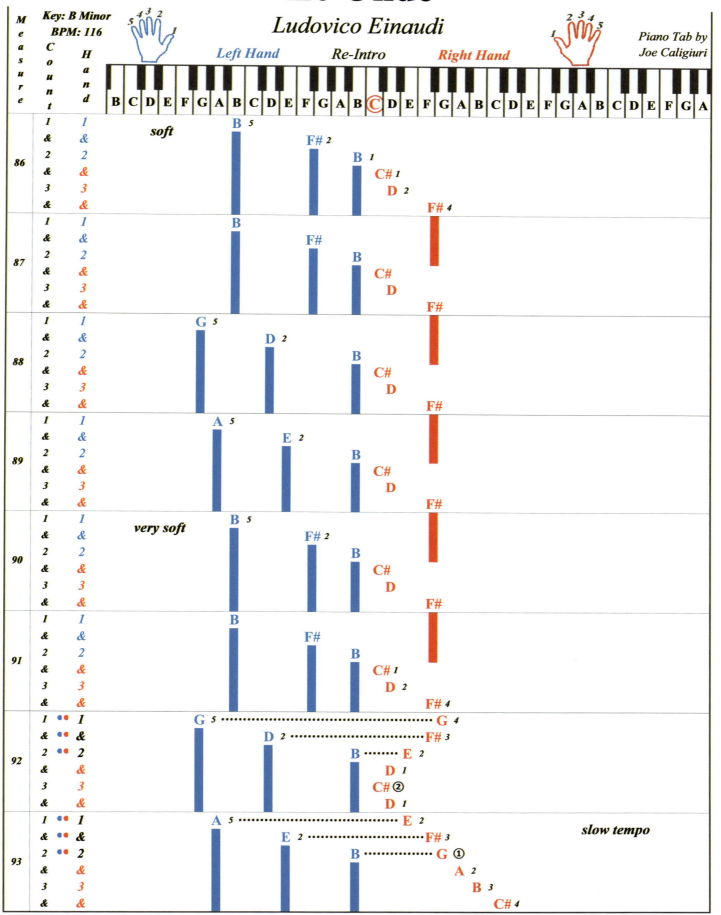

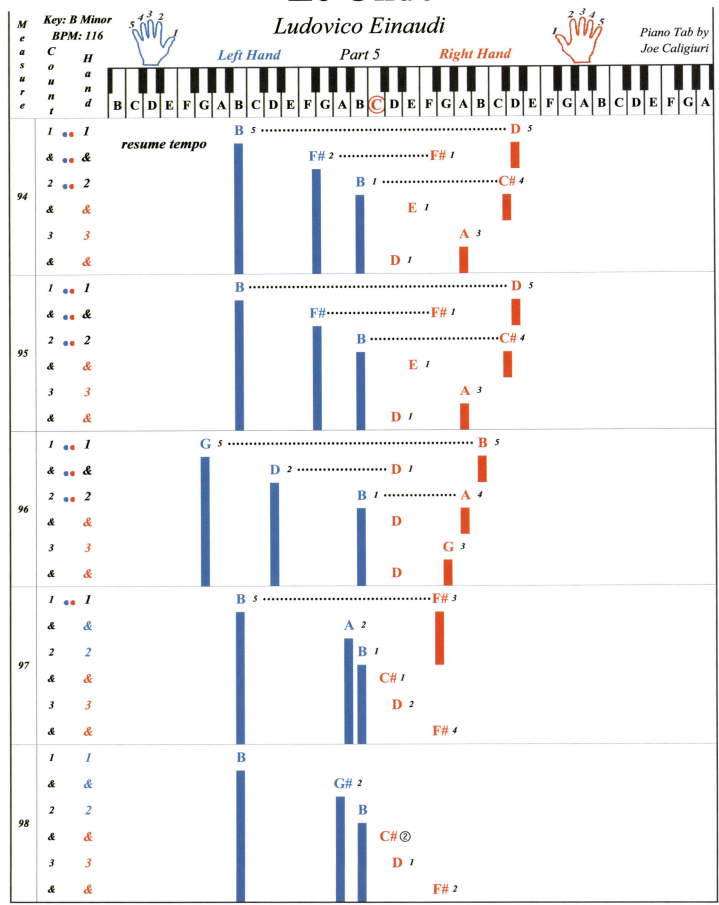

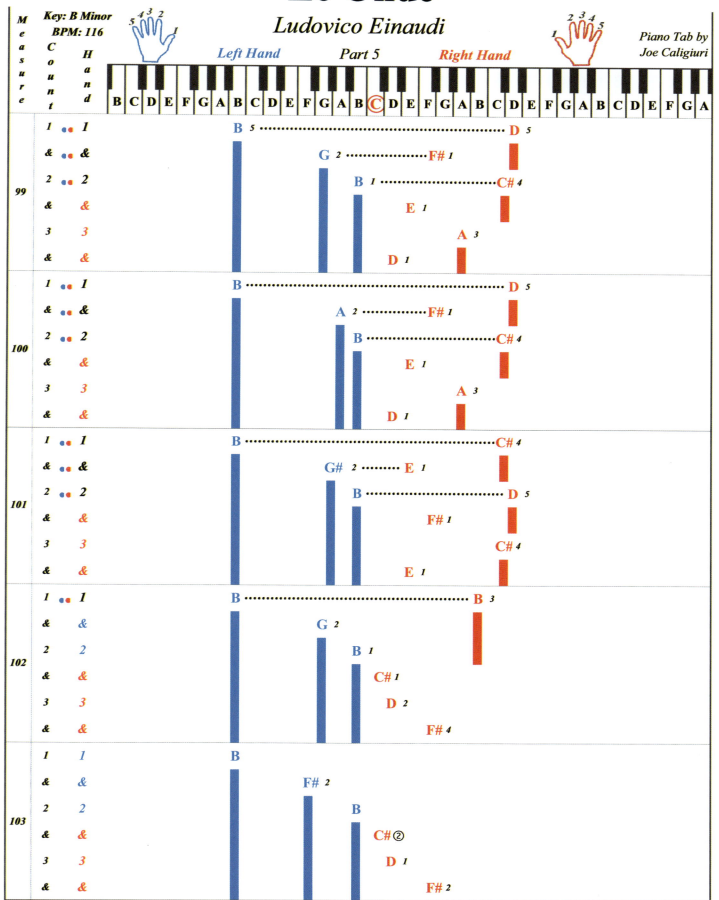

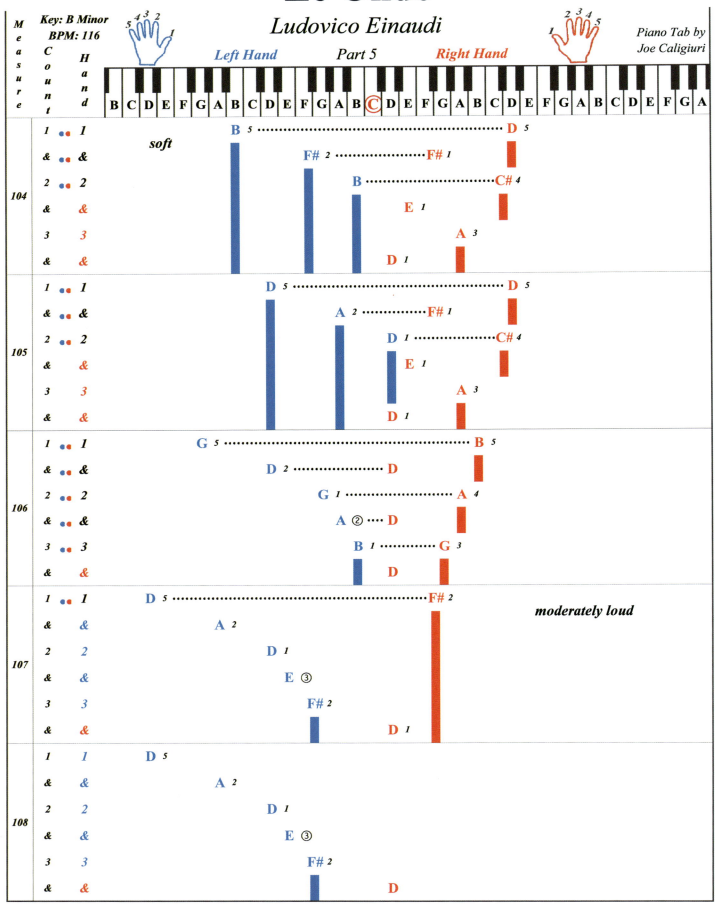

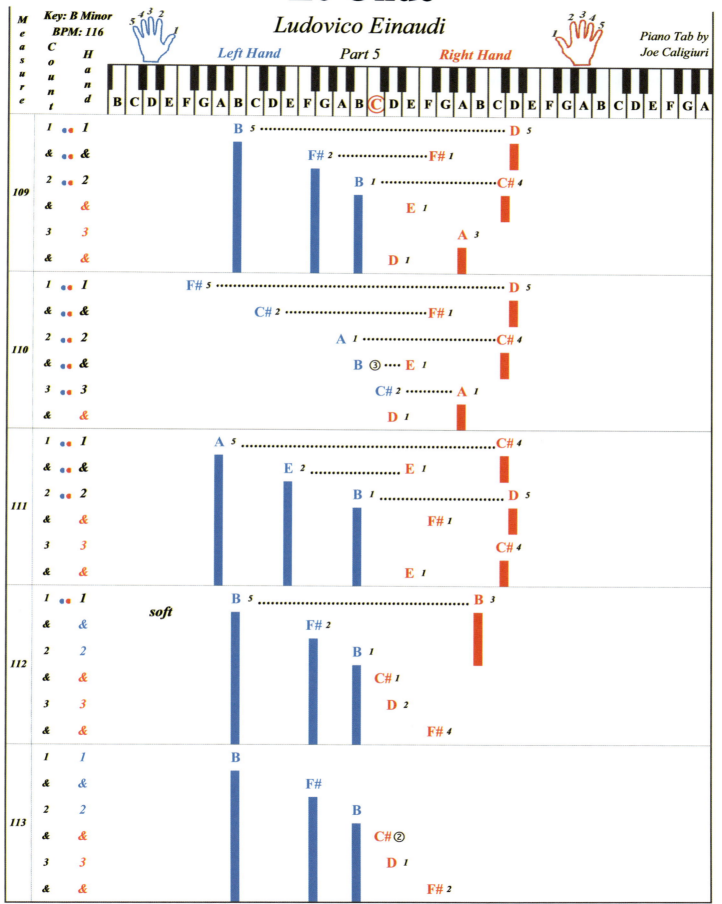

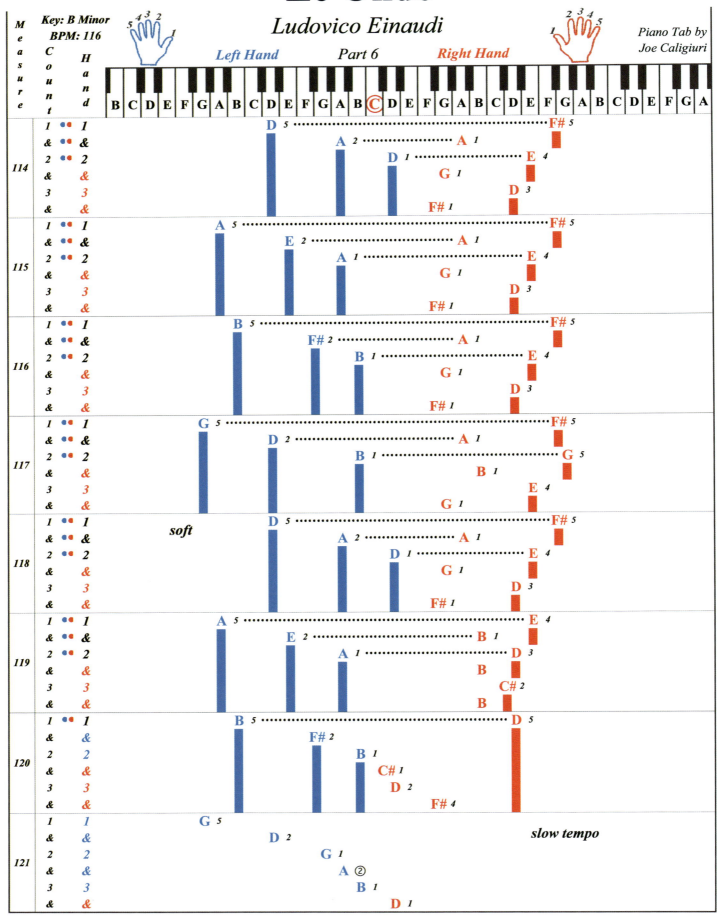

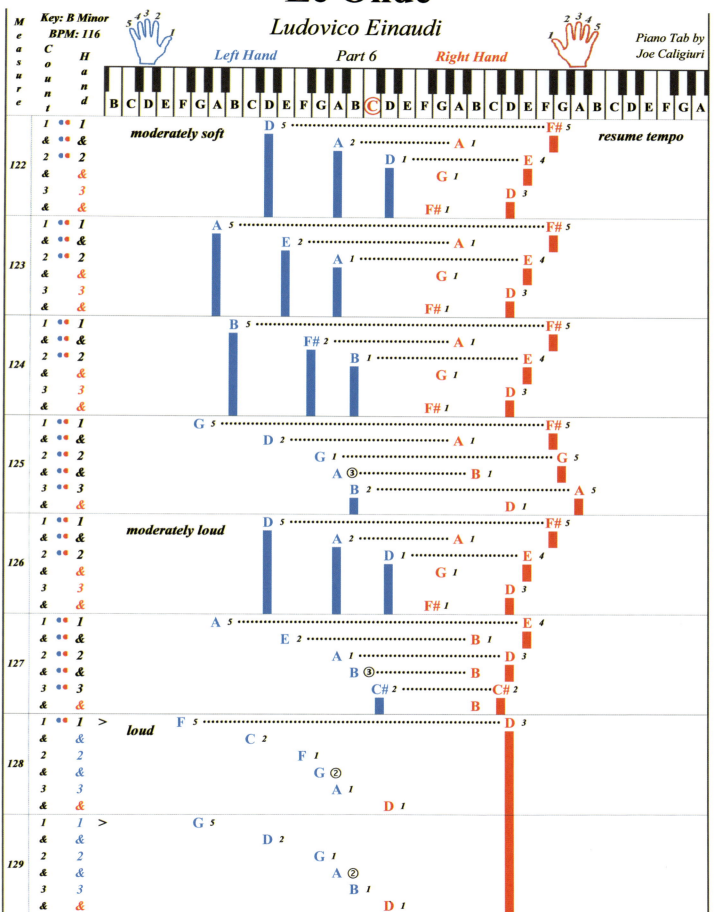

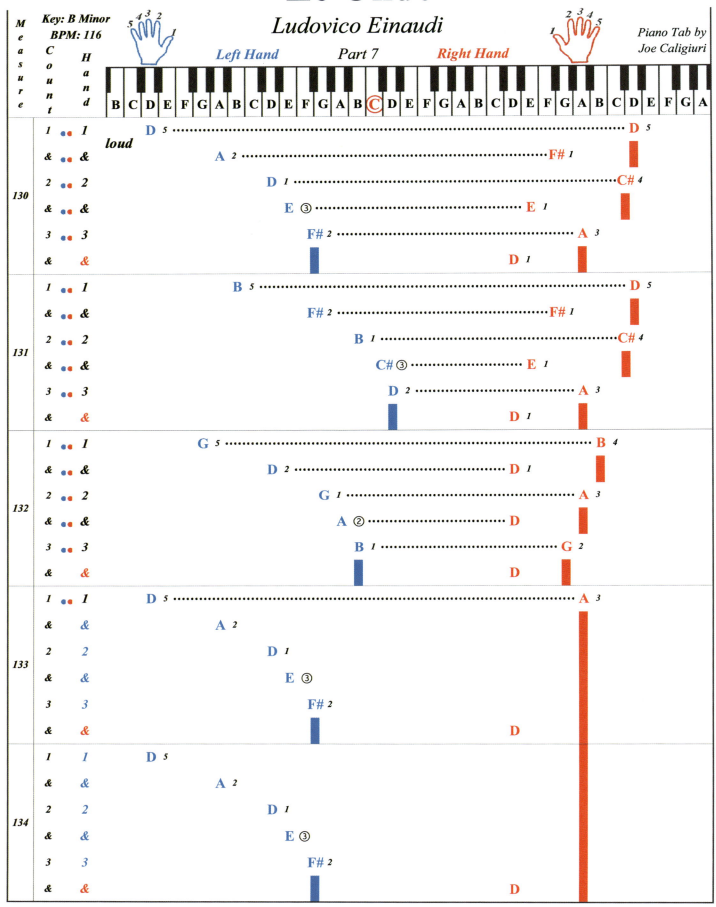

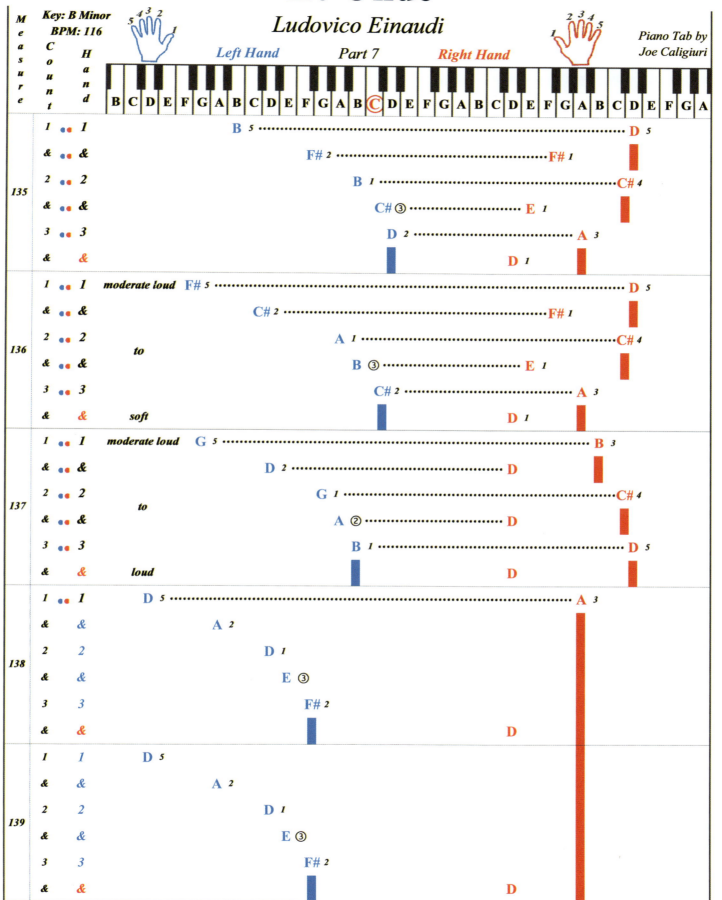

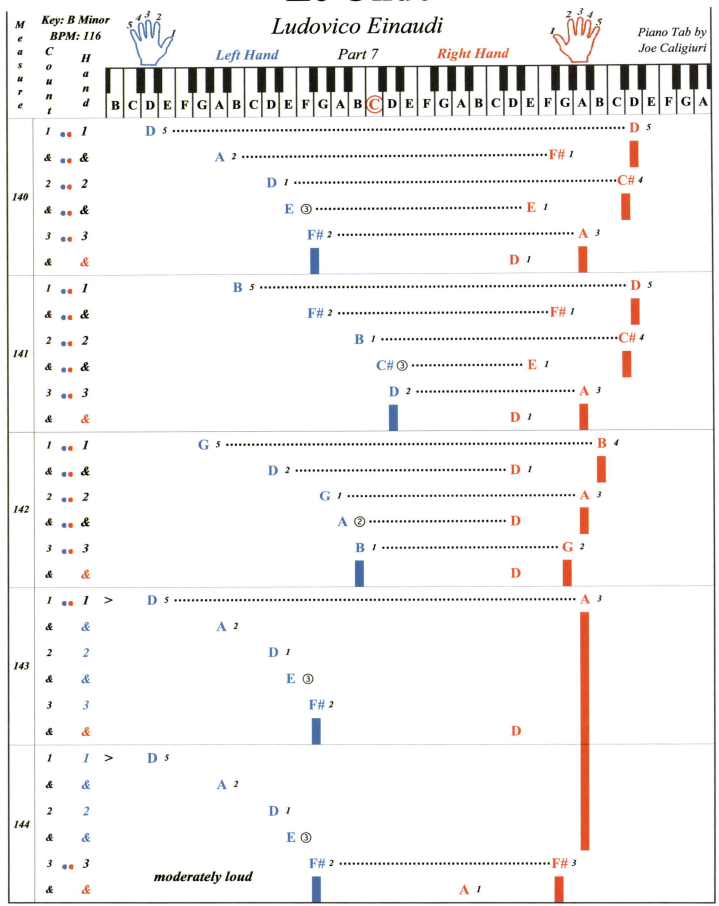

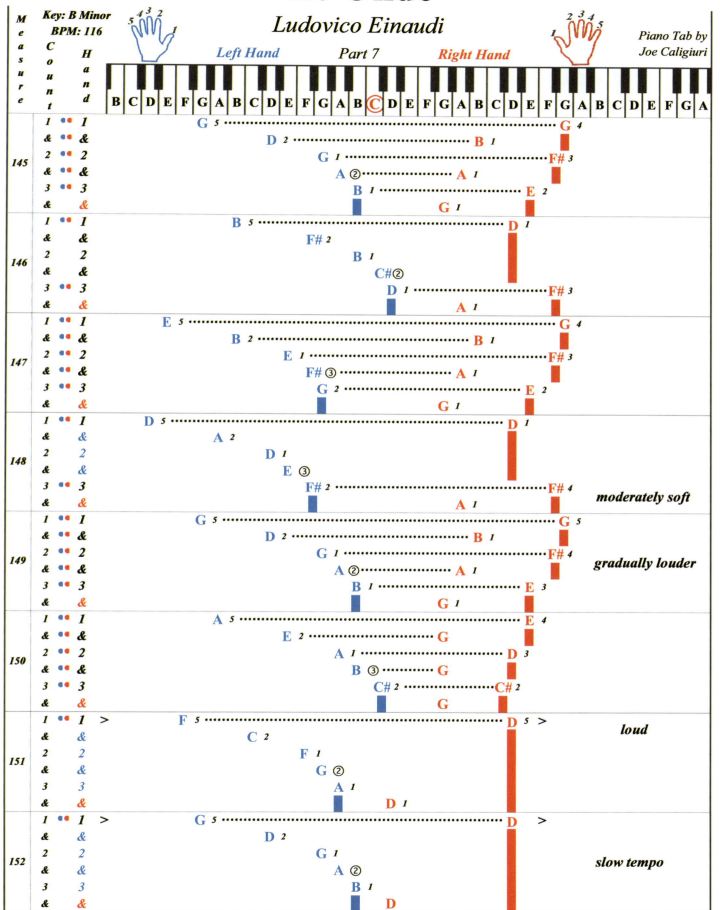

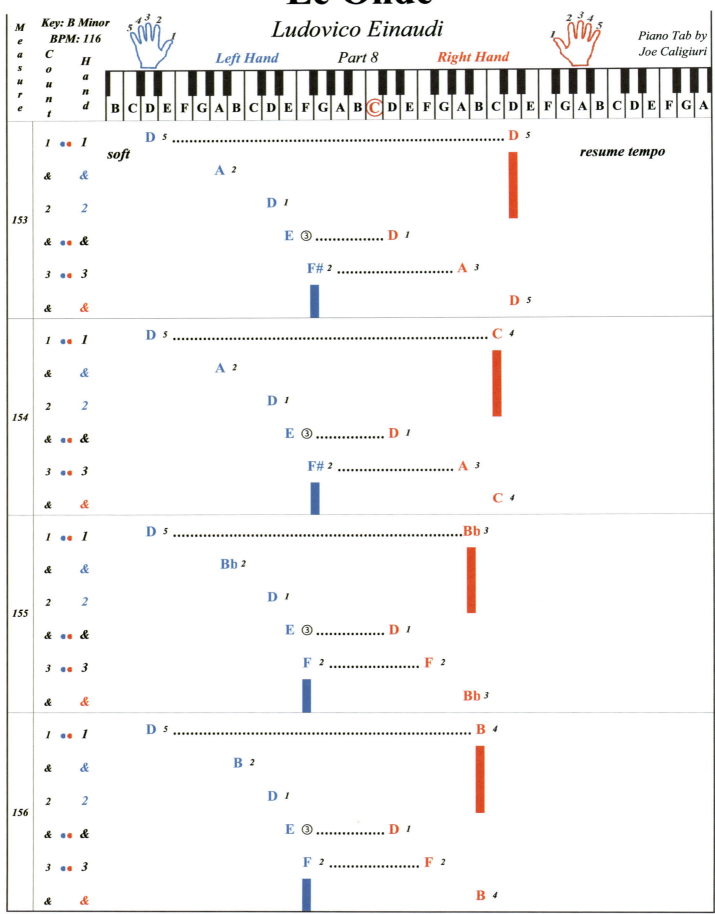

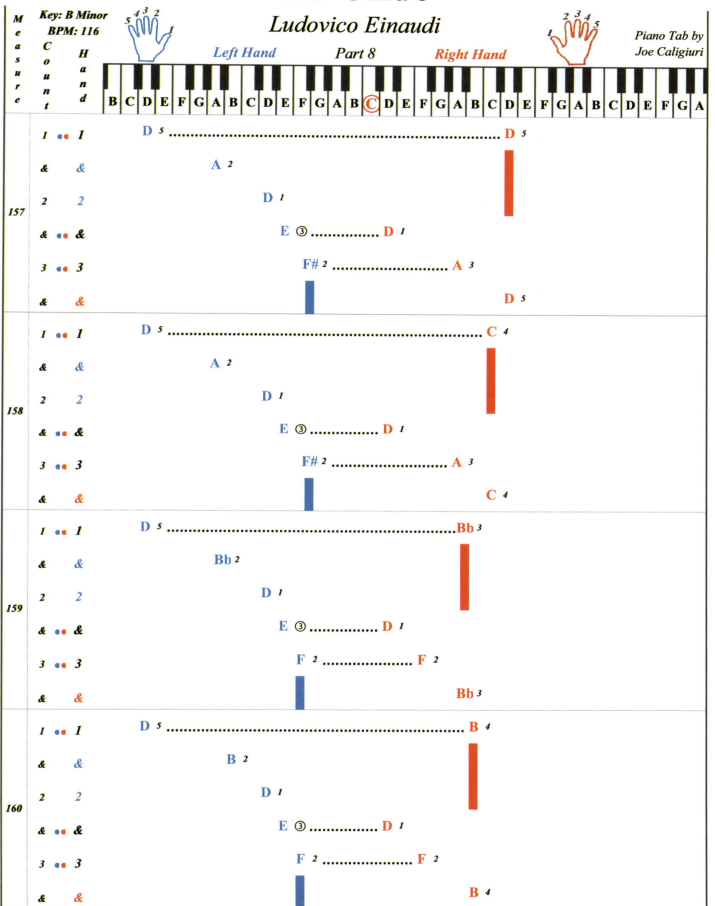

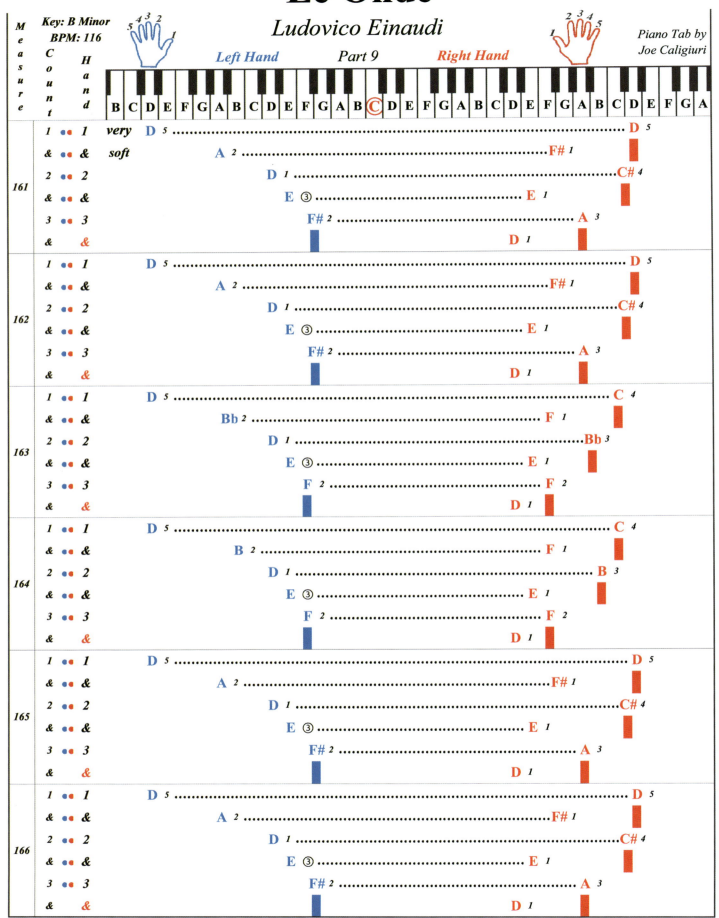

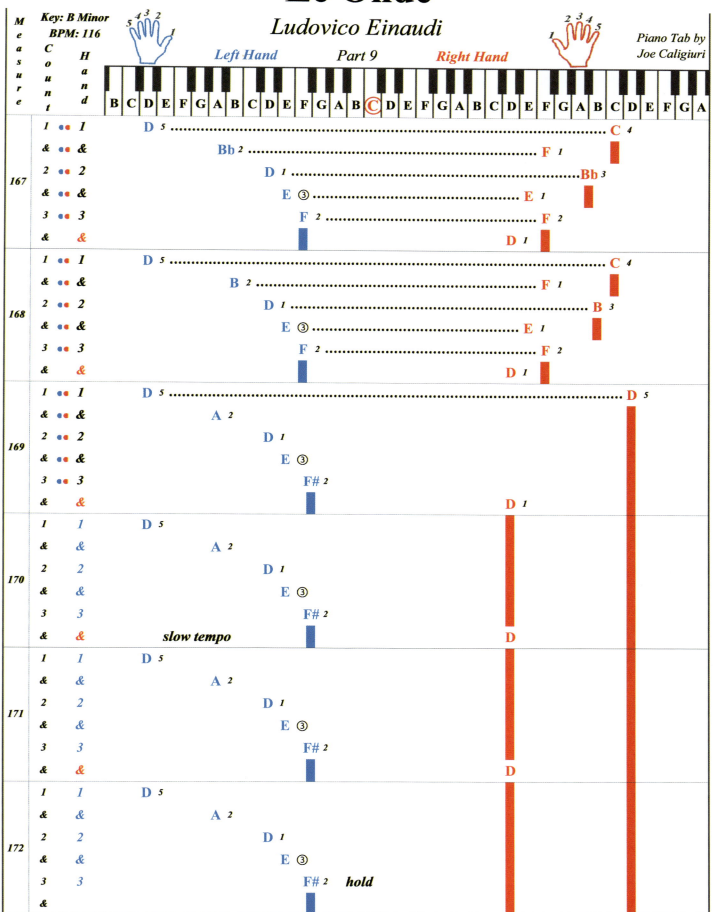

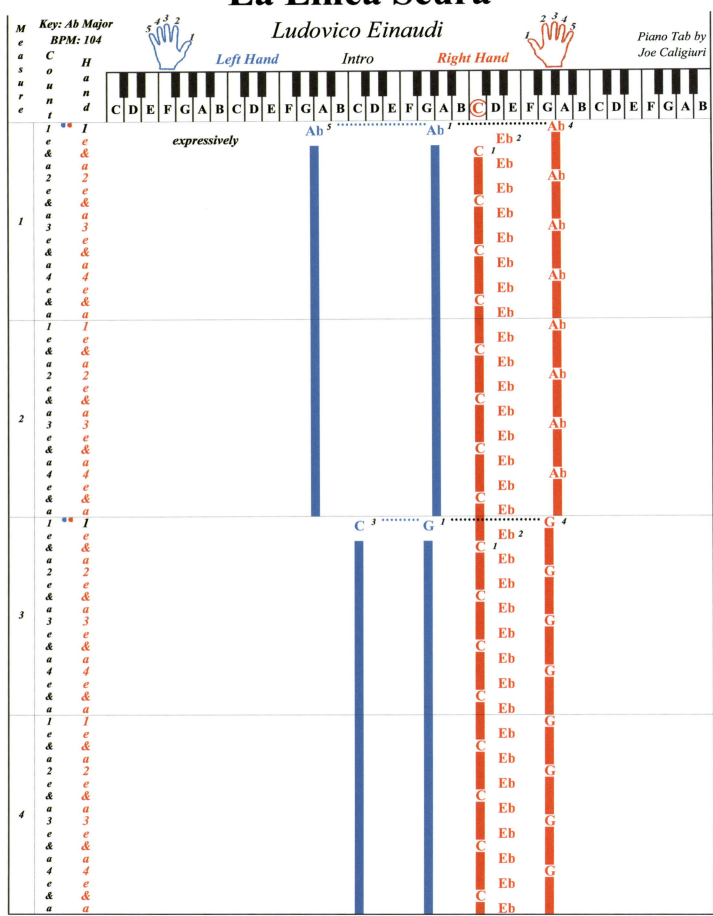

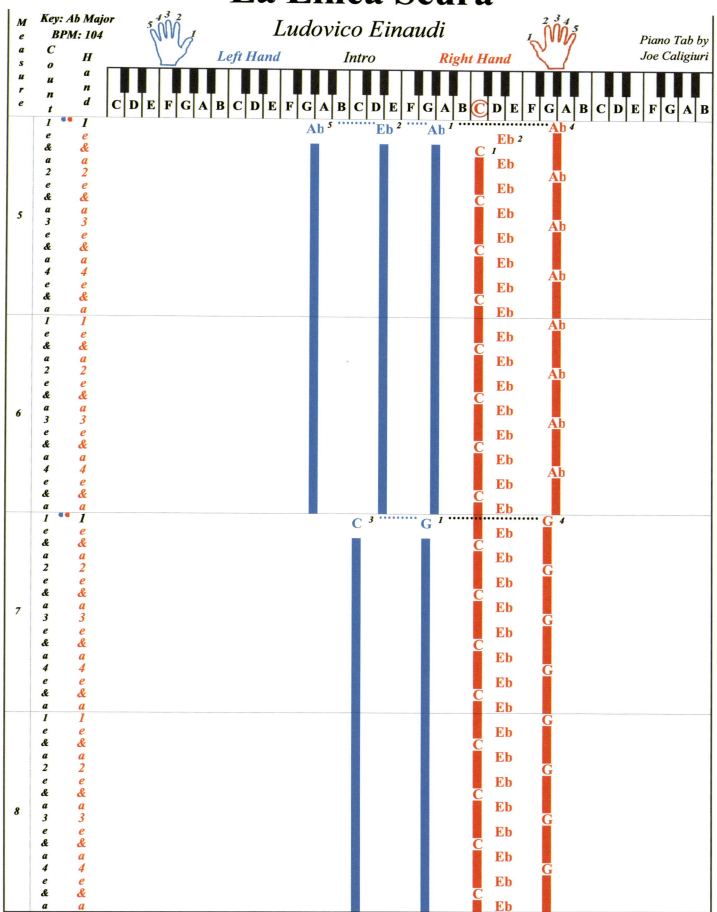

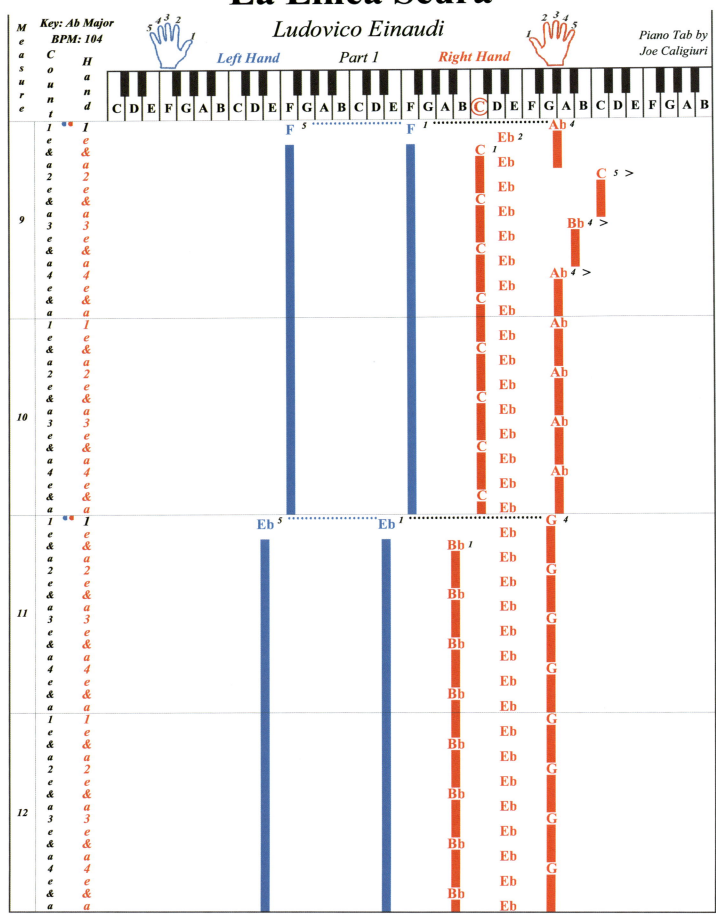

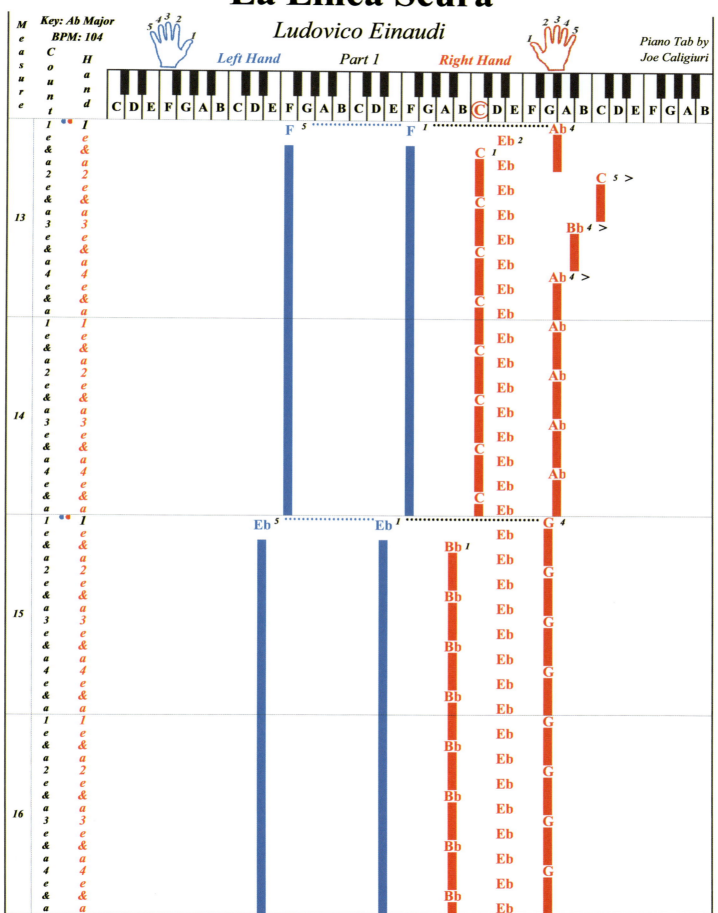

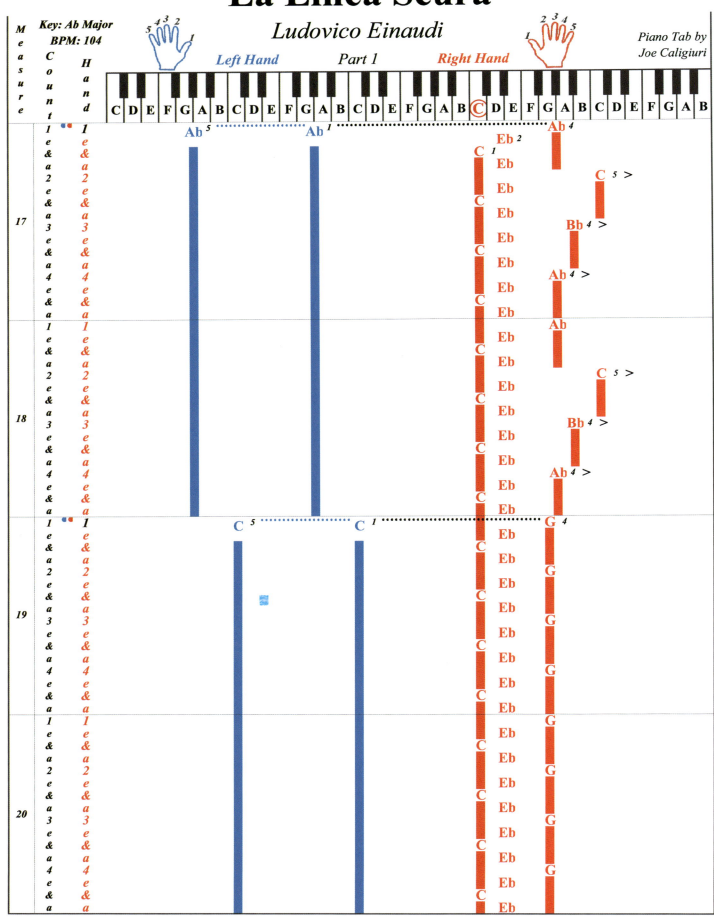

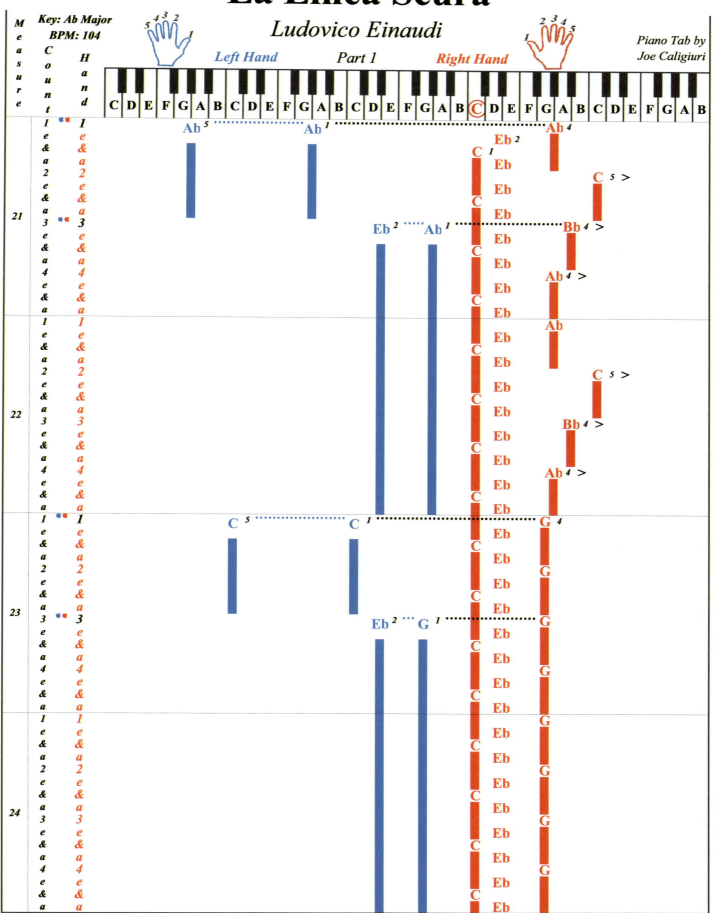

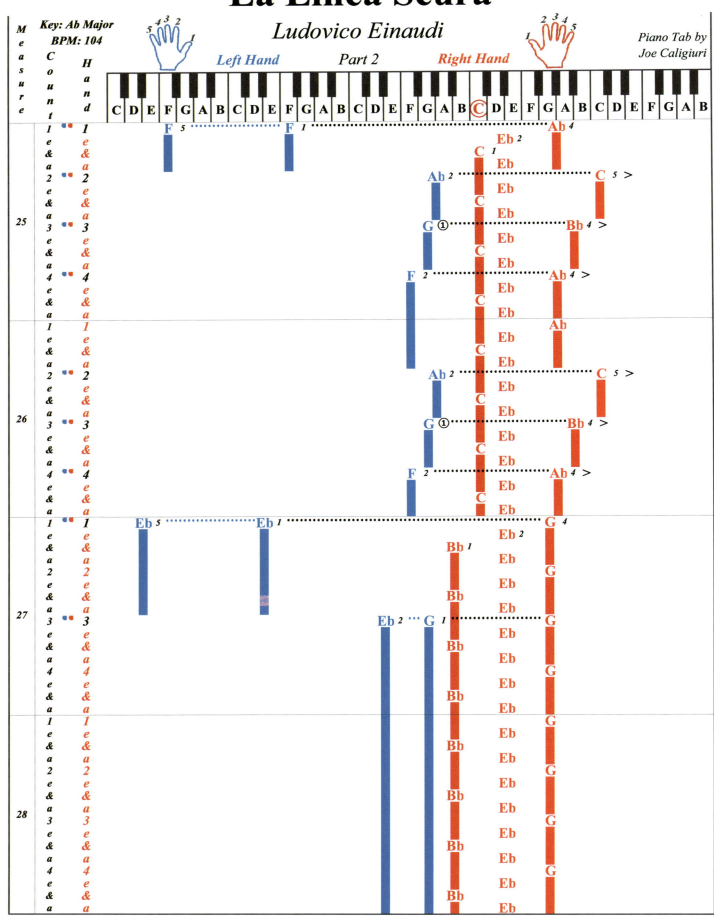

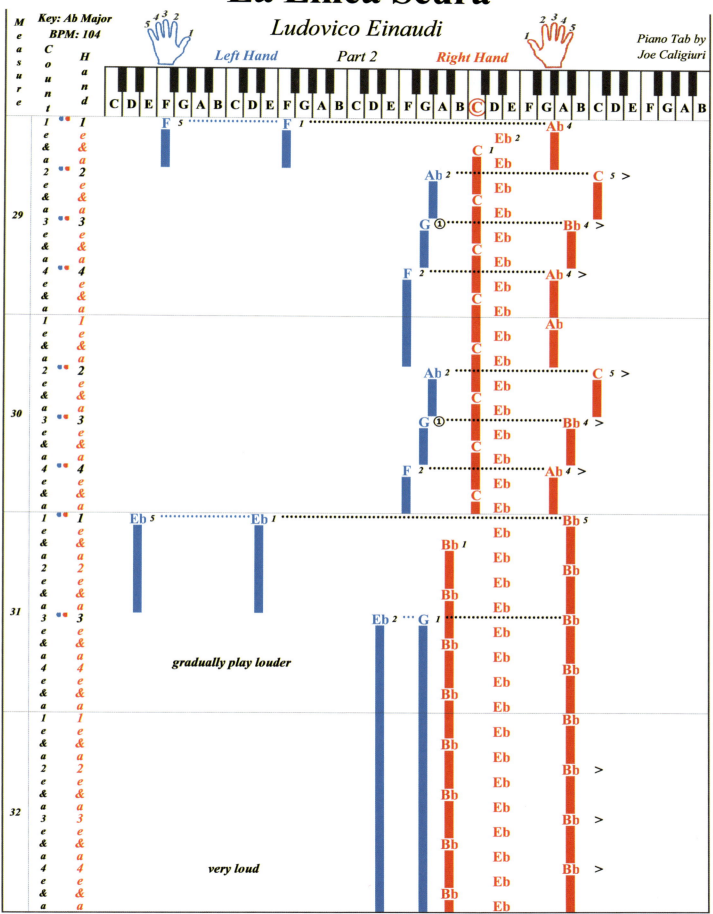

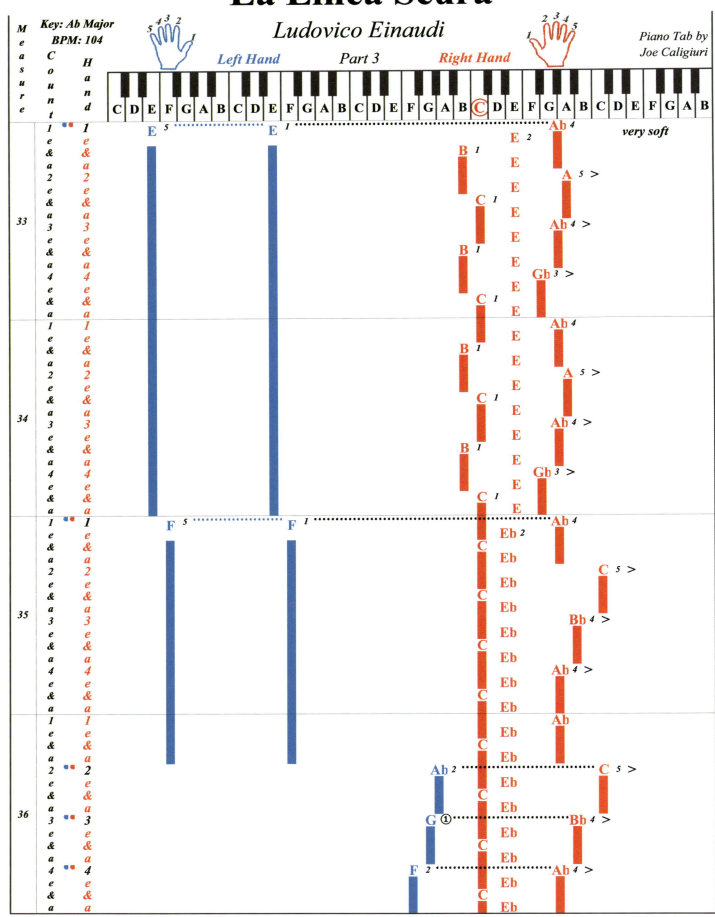

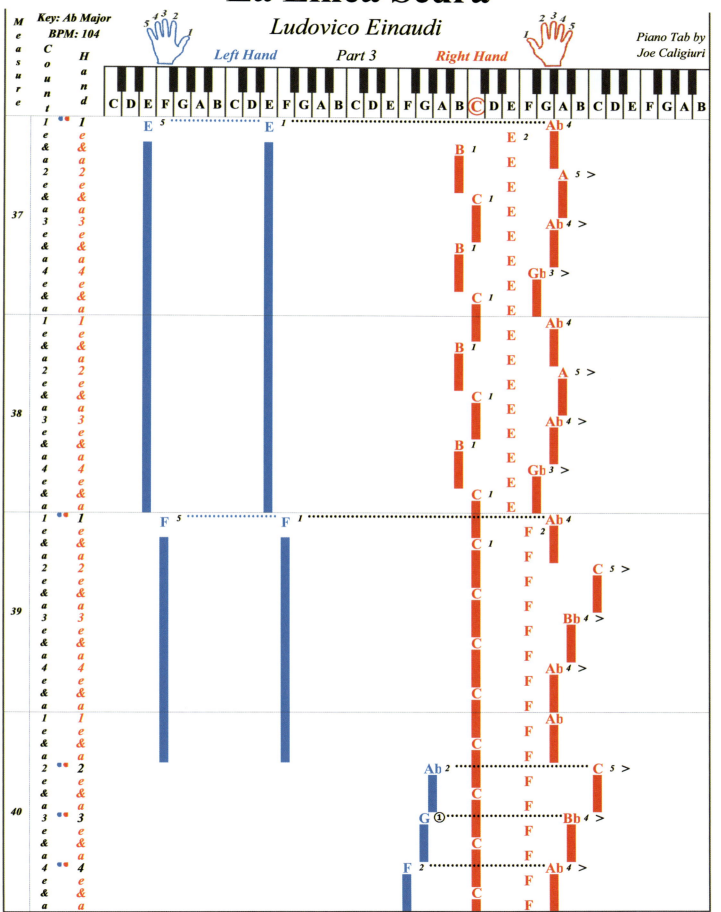

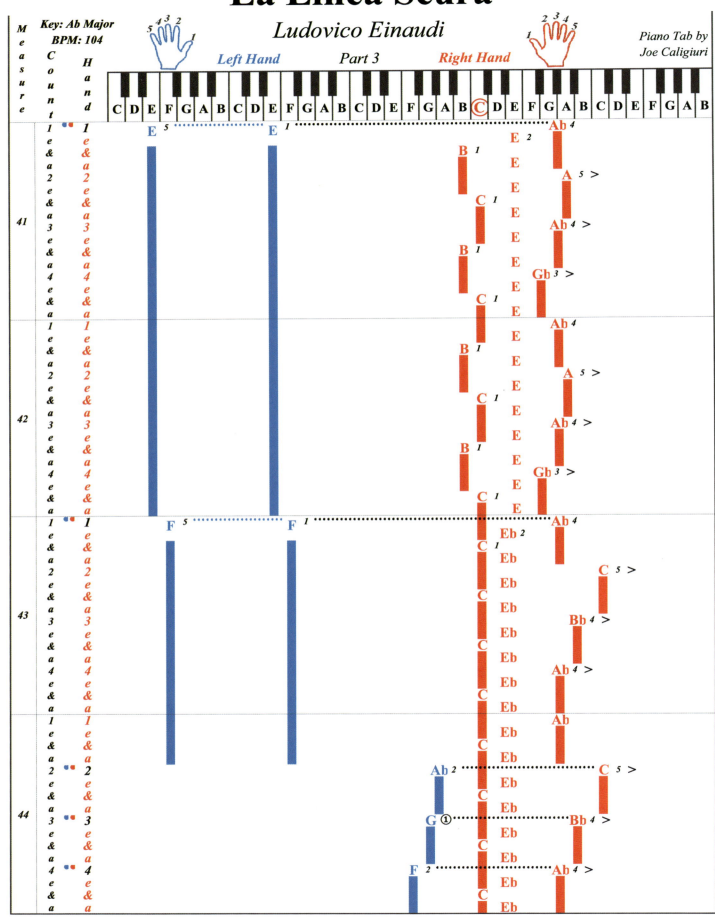

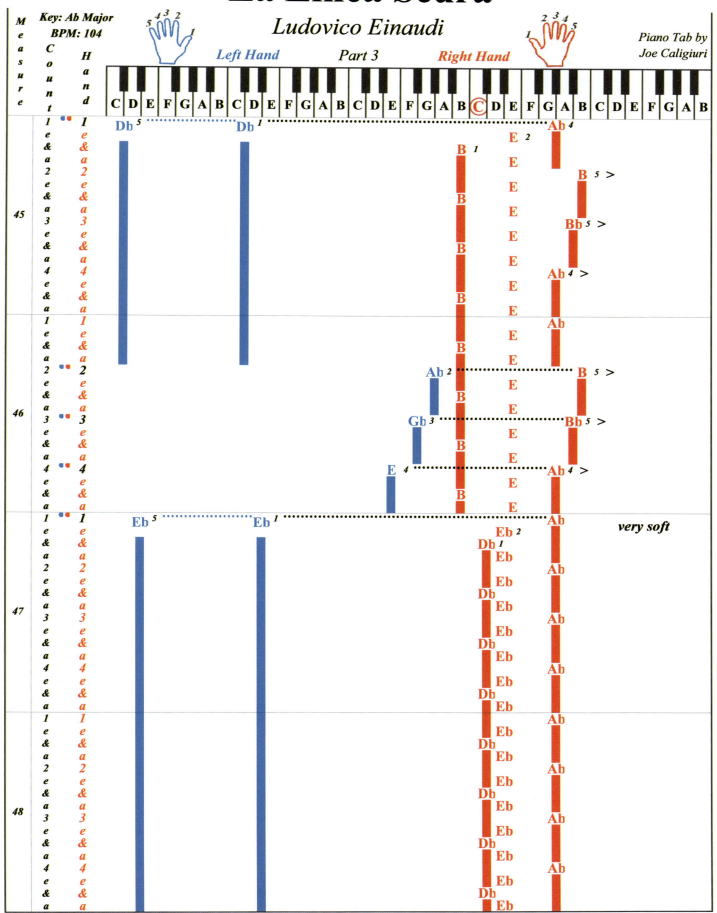

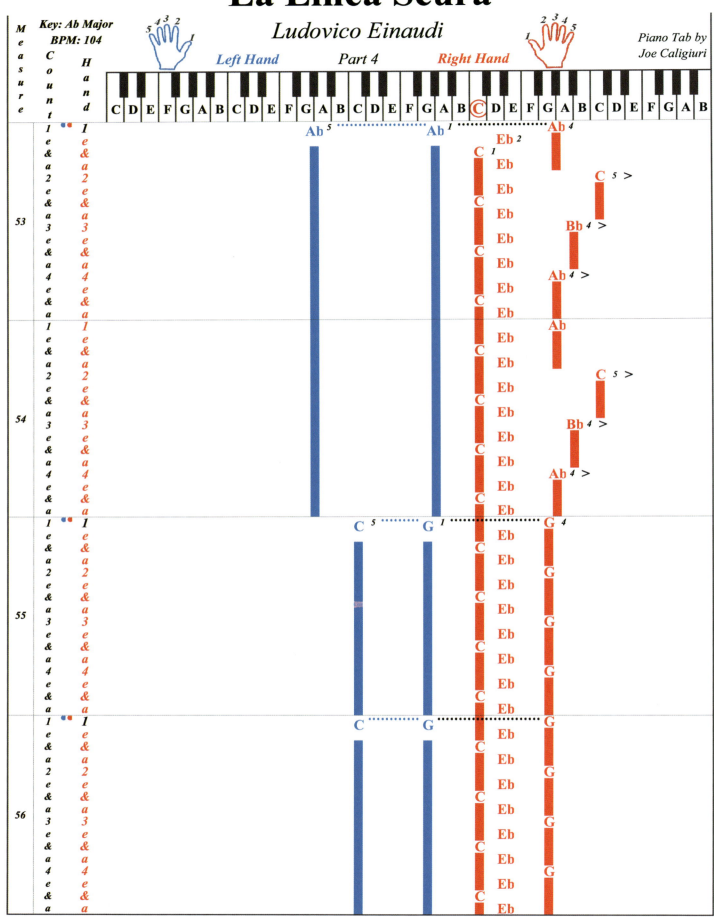

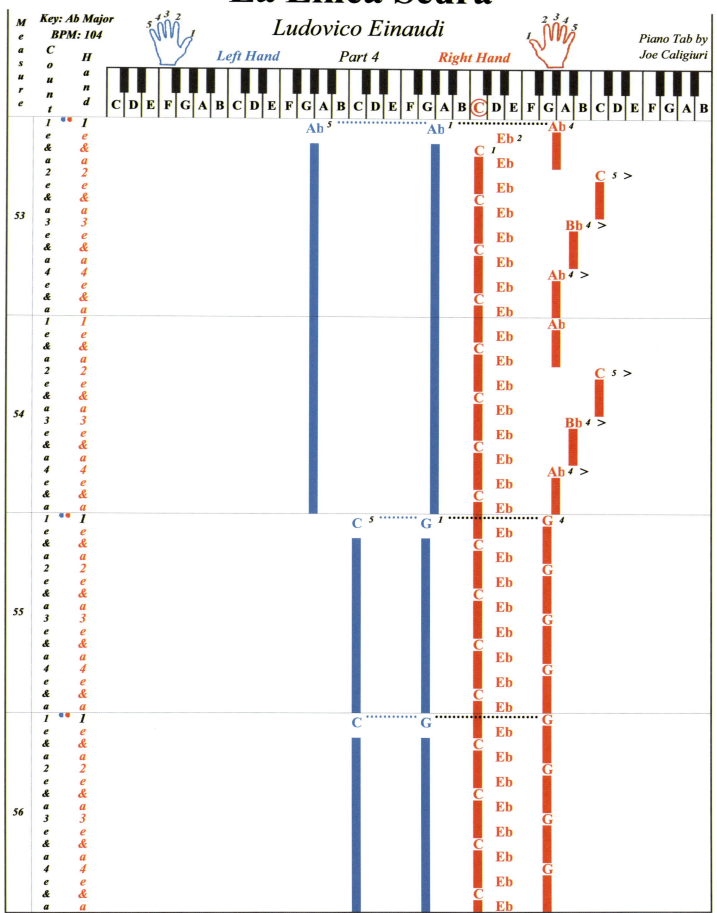

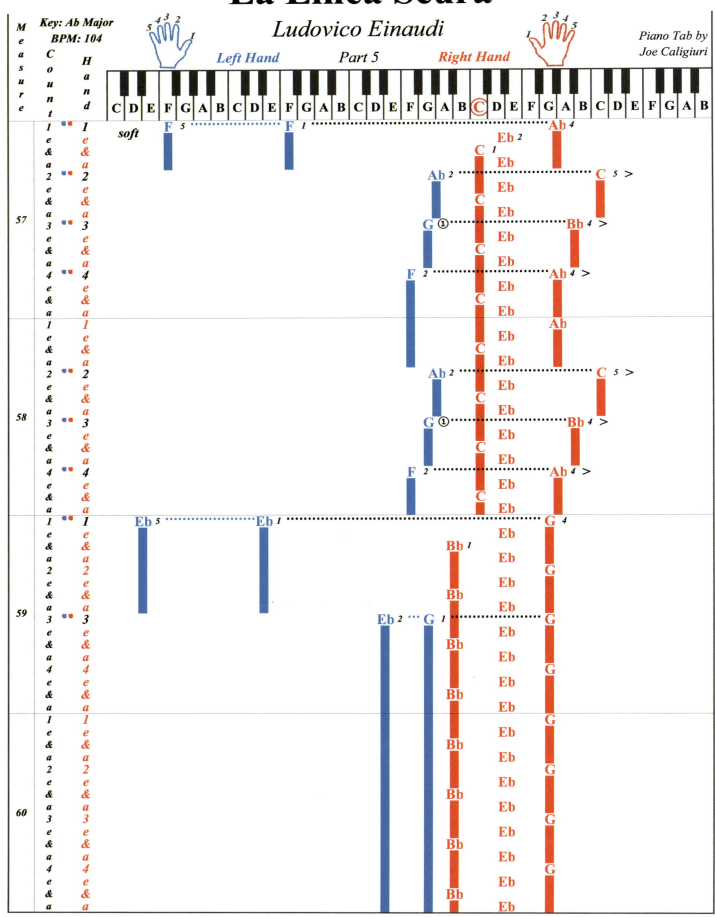

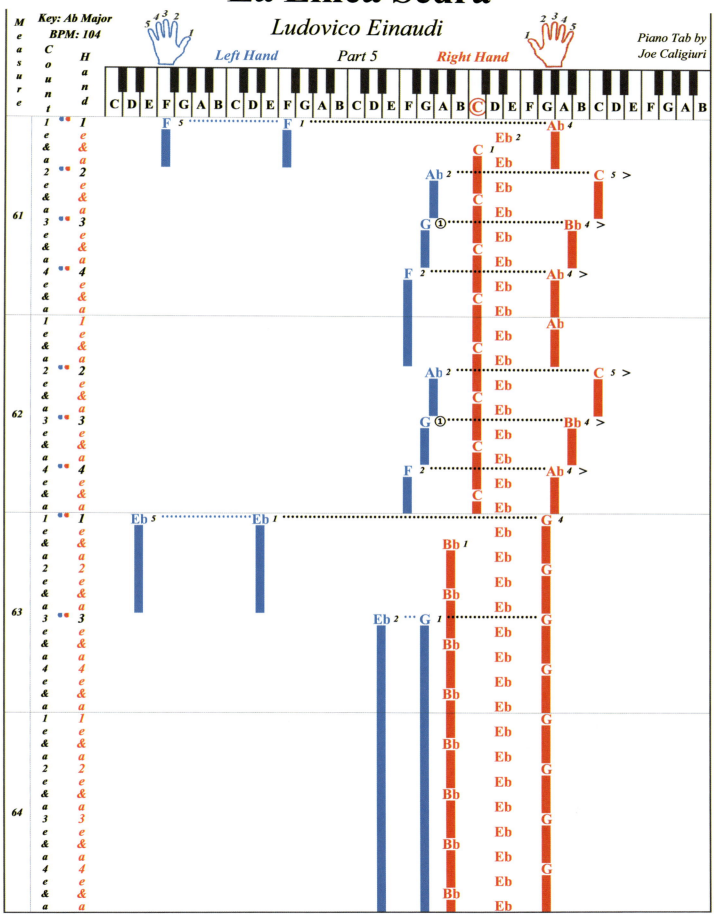

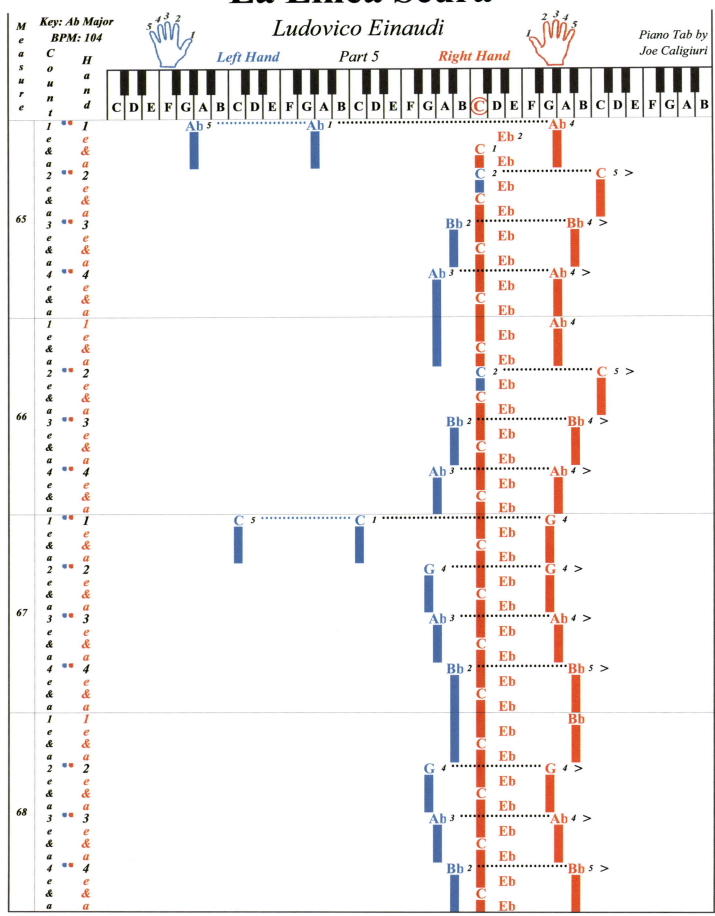

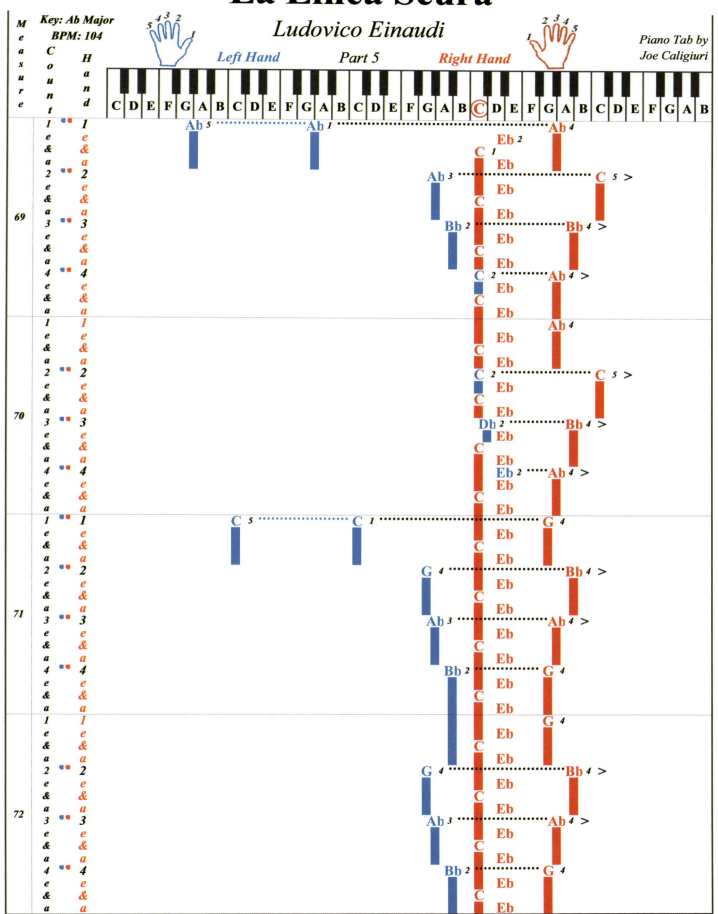

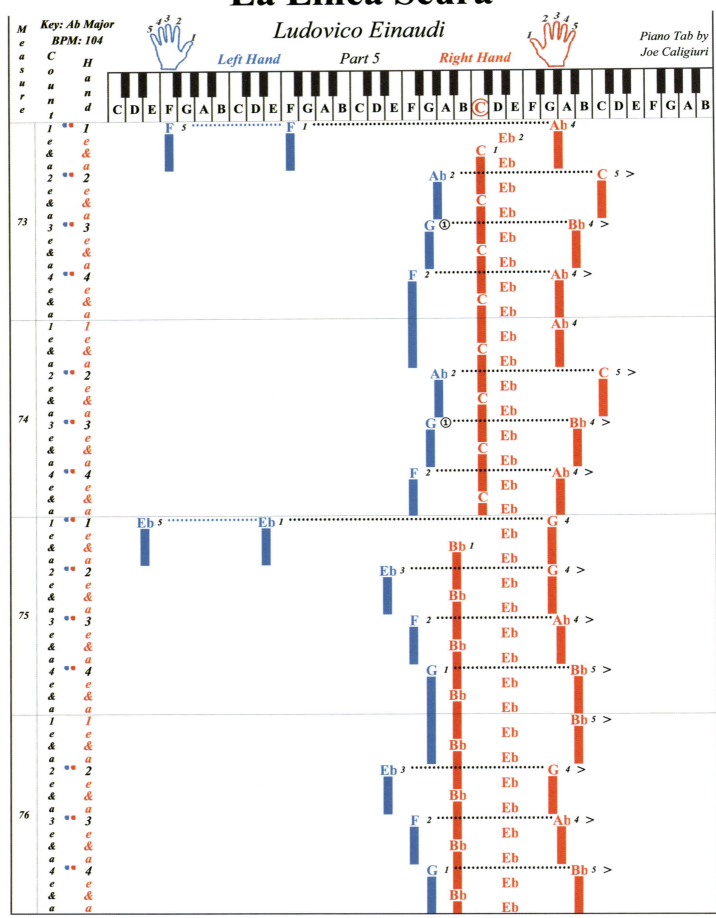

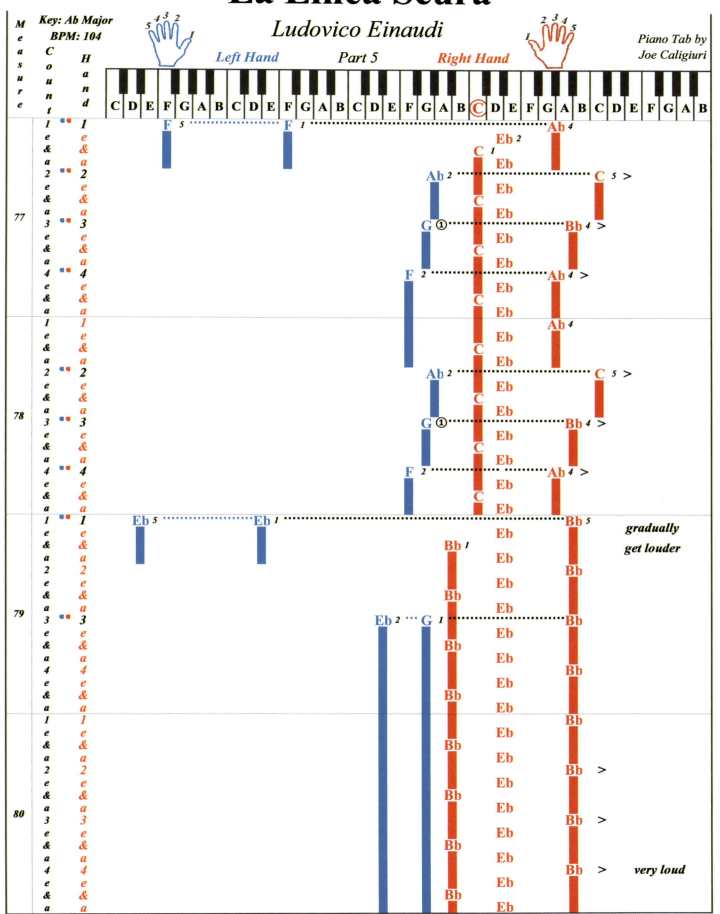

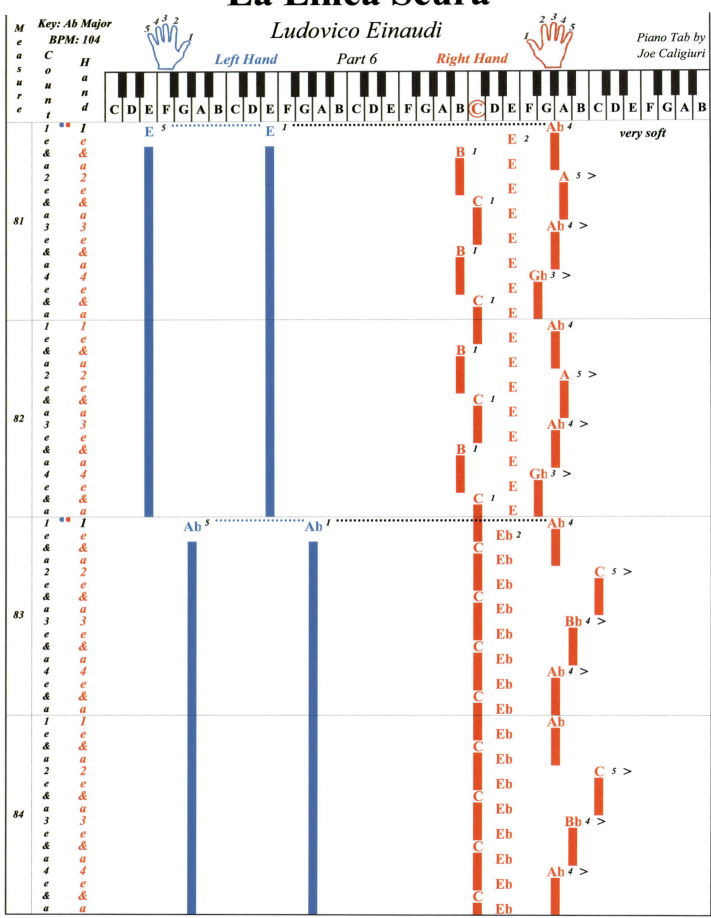

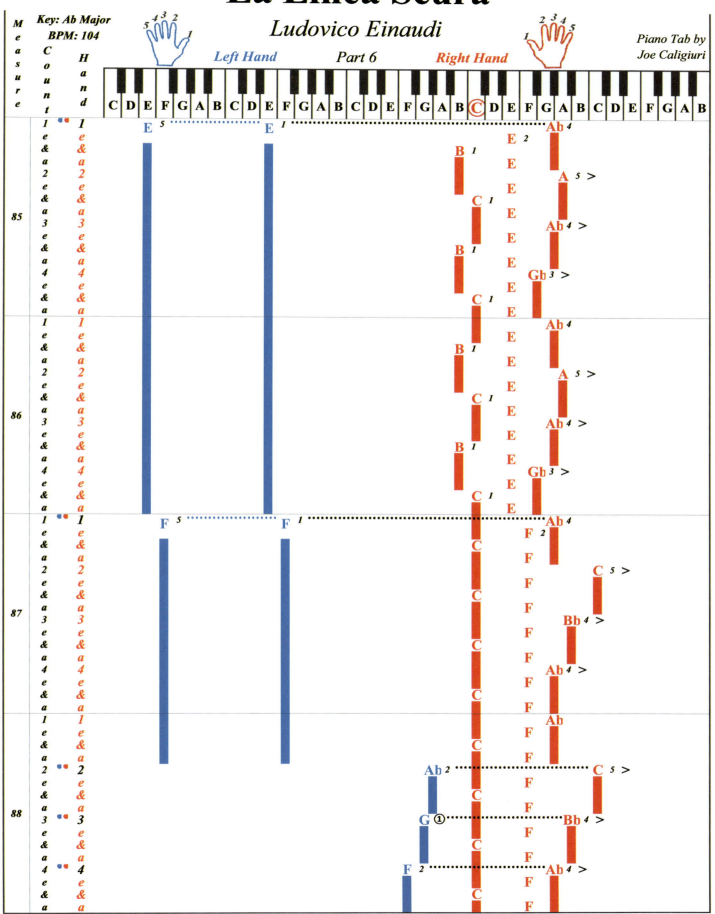

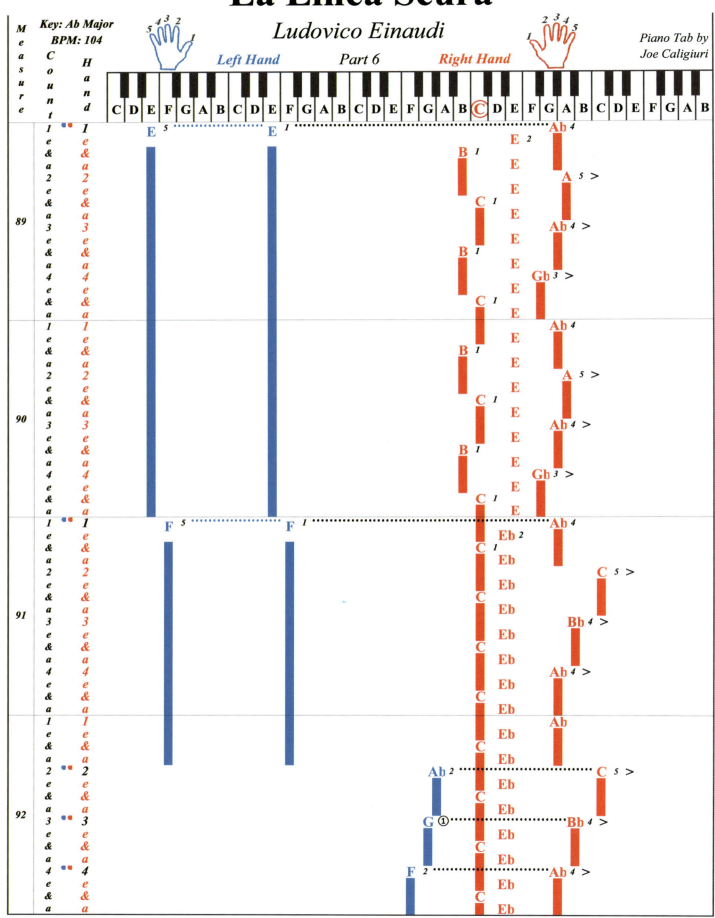

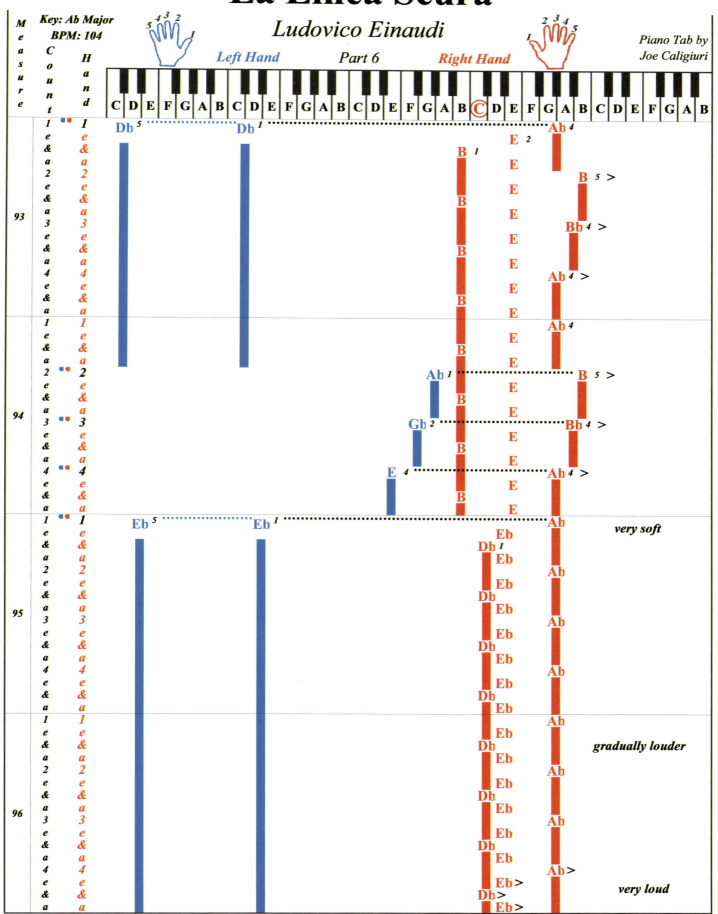

Also Available at Amazon.com & PlayPianoByLetters.com

 28 Songs 73 Pages

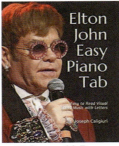 15 Songs 93 Pages

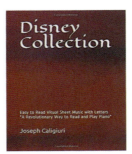 24 Songs 77 Pages

 42 Songs 125 Pages

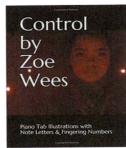 Whole Song 25 Pages

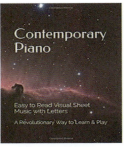 26 Songs 126 Pages

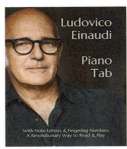 18 Songs 203 Pages

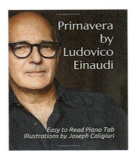 Whole Song 31 Pages

 Whole Song 35 Pages

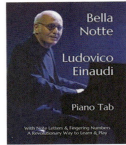 Whole Song 29 Pages

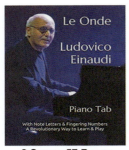 2 Songs 57 Pages

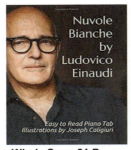 Whole Song 31 Pages

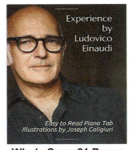 Whole Song 31 Pages

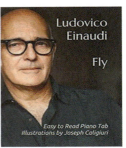 Whole Song 27 Pages

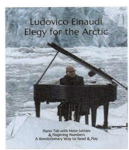 Whole Song 25 Pages

 32 Songs 125 Pages

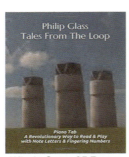 Whole Song 25 Pages

 50 Songs 75 Pages

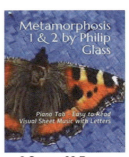 2 Songs 32 Pages

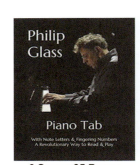 6 Songs 35 Pages

 5 Songs 34 Pages

 Whole Song 27 Pages

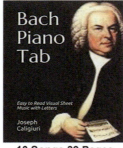 10 Songs 39 Pages

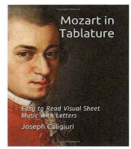 7 Songs 28 Pages

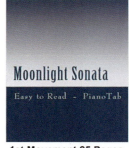 1st Movement 25 Pages

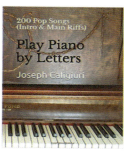				
200 Songs 291 Pages	**7 Songs 73 Pages**	**10 Songs 33 Pages**	**5 Songs 75 Pages**	**30 Songs 123 Pages**
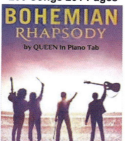	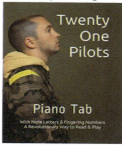	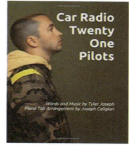	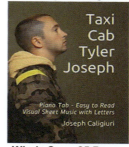	
Whole Song 30 Pages	**21 Songs 147 Pages**	**Whole Song 25 Pages**	**Whole Song 25 Pages**	**Whole Song 25 Pages**
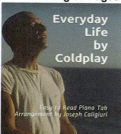	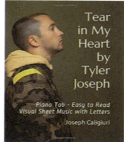	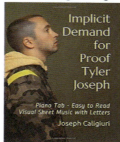		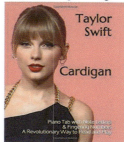
Whole Song 27 Pages	**Whole Song 25 Pages**	**Whole Song 29 Pages**	**Whole Song 29 Pages**	**Whole Song 27 Pages**
	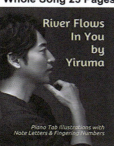		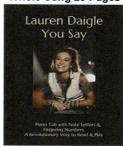	
Whole Song 32 Pages	**Whole Song 27 Pages**	**Whole Song 29 Pages**	**Whole Song 25 Pages**	**6 Songs 79 Pages**
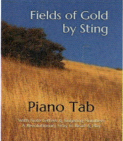	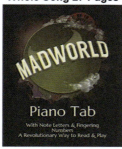	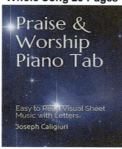	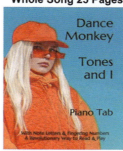	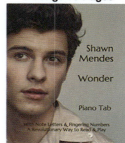
Whole Song 35 Pages	**Whole Song 27 Pages**	**19 Songs 61 Pages**	**Whole Song 33 Pages**	**Whole Song 29 Pages**
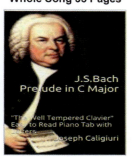			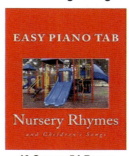	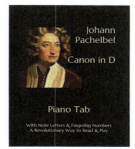
Kindle eBook 5 Pages	**Whole Song 27 Pages**	**25 Songs 64 Pages**	**40 Songs 54 Pages**	**Whole Song 25 Pages**

Printed in Great Britain
by Amazon